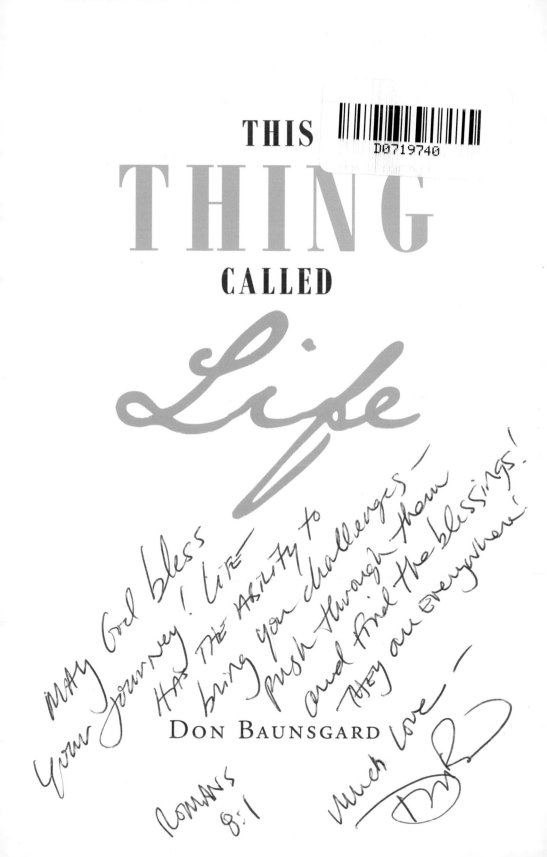

THIS
THING
CALLED
Life

DON BAUNSGARD

MAy God bless your journey! Life— HAS THE ABILITY to bring you challenges— push through them and find the blessings! THEY are Everywhere!

ROMANS 8:1

Much Love

ISBN 978-1-64300-635-2 (Paperback)
ISBN 978-1-64300-636-9 (Digital)

Covenant Books, Inc.
11661 Hwy 707
Murrells Inlet, SC 29576
www.covenantbooks.com

To my wife, Lena, who always believed in me.

CONTENTS

I have first- hand seen the effects of giving and it is more beautiful than I could have ever imagined. It truly is better to give than to receive. I only want to give more. What else can I do to change these children's lives? What else can I sacrifice? What else can I let go of? What else? I know I can do more and it is up to me! Take that step of faith—step in the direction of Christ and store up more treasures in heaven. I know God is smiling down on me. I know He is happy. I only want to continue to shine for my Lord and Savior. I love you Jesus!

—Don Baunsgard
Nov 6, 2006, Kasitu, Uganda

CHAPTER 1

You Have Chosen . . . *Wisely*

May your choices reflect your hopes not your fears.
—Nelson Mandela

There are moments when one has to choose between
living one's own life fully, entirely, completely . . .
Or . . . dragging out some false, shallow, degrading
existence that the world in its hypocrisy demands.
—Oscar Wilde

I have loved movies for as long as I can remember. I love how movies can take us to other worlds and on new adventures. They make us laugh, cry, and experience every other emotion, touching on almost every subject. We are quickly transported out of our reality into this great adventure, or they take us back into history to give us a glimpse of what it must have looked like or felt like through some of the most dramatic times of our existence.

It will become quite obvious to you, throughout these chapters, that movies have impacted my life greatly. I believe there is a lot we can learn from them, but I also believe they can hold a deeper message that is trying to be revealed through many different angles and throughout the story being told. I can still remember when I was eight years old, in a galaxy far, far away, my dad took my brothers and me to see *Star Wars* for the first time at the drive-in theater. Like everyone else who was watching this movie for the first time, I was mesmerized by the effects and the story of the characters involved, and I have often found myself relating to the characters in movies and the challenges they have to overcome.

Steven Spielberg is probably, and most rightly so, my favorite director and storyteller. One of his most memorable characters, which actually was created by George Lucas, is in the movie *Indiana Jones and the Last Crusade*, the third installment of the *Raiders of the Lost Ark* franchise. Indiana is again on a journey to find a Holy Relic . . . the Holy Grail. But, this time, he is trying to save his father's life, and the Holy Grail holds the power to heal his father's deadly gunshot wound. With just a drop of water from this holy cup, which was supposedly the cup used by Jesus of Nazareth at the Last Supper, his wound would miraculously heal.

Through many perilous riddles, taking a huge leap of faith and narrowly escaping death several times, he weaves his way through the challenges set before him until he finally arrives at his final destination—the cave with the Holy Grail inside. Upon entering this cave, it eventually leads to a room where he finds a brave old knight who has been standing guard for centuries protecting the Holy Grail. The challenge of finding the Holy Grail in this room is that along with it are hundreds of other chalices, glasses, and bowls that all could be the *one* Holy Grail. So here lies the problem, Indy has to figure out which one is truly "The One," and if he chooses the wrong one, his father dies and so does he and his friends. So, looking at them all, Indy finally chooses an old looking wooden or ceramic glass amongst the many other more vibrant and beautiful options, all the while, his dad is slowly dying and he is running out of time. Then in dramatic fashion . . . the old knight says to Indy, "You have chosen . . . *Wisely*." Without wasting any time, Indy quickly dips the chalice into the water basin, pours it on his dad's wound, and saves his dad! They ride off into the sunset with their friends happily ever after. Love that movie!

Sometimes, the choices we have to make are life-changing or will have a huge impact on our lives going forward. And then, there

Family Rules
Help Each Other
Always Tell the Truth
Share
doyourbest
Pay with Hugs and Kisses
Listen to your Parents
Laugh at Yourself
Say I Love You
Try New Things
Be Thankful
Show Compassion
Be Happy
Love Each Other
Dream Big
Respect One Another
Laugh Out Loud
Keep Your Promises
Say Please and Thank
You
B e G r a t e f u l
Think of Others Before Yourself
Use Kind Words
Know You Are Loved
Hug Often

are the choices that we make that we had no idea would change everything about our current lives and all that we thought they would be. (Insert children here.)

Choices are a part of our every day, every minute life. We can't ignore them, and we can't run from them. They simply have to be made. Some choices are minor, and some take days to make. However, we have control over our choices. What we eat, what we think, what we say, where we go and what we will do with our lives . . . *but choose wisely*.

You have the power to change who you are and the power to change the world and everything in it. You can also make a difference in someone's life if you so choose to. Everything you decide to do will, in one way or another, have a direct impact on your life, the people around you and the world, good or bad. It is up to each of us to decide how and when we are going to choose wisely.

As a child, we soon learn how choices impact us, and as we grow older, our choices change, and we soon realize that it is up to each of us to determine what direction we want to go. Don't ever underestimate the power of your choices. Realize also that your choices can, and ultimately will, define who you are choosing to become.

My wife and I strongly believe in positive reinforcement. Throughout our house, we have many different signs with positive words of truth, love, and encouragement.

The sign on the previous page is hung in our dining room.

Each of these suggestions become choices we make that will bring light and love into both the lives of those whom you love and into your very heart. We try as a family to make sure we are reading this out loud before we start dinner most evenings. The more you believe in these words, the more you will act on them. They will become a part of your DNA and your everyday life. When you start to understand how much these words mean and the amount of love that is in them, you will want to help incorporate them into your children's lives and put them into action.

I have always made an attempt to be a person who exemplifies the light and love of Jesus—to be light in this world. To choose to lift people up and not bring them down. I have long believed that it is so very important to make people feel valued, worthy and loved. To try and find the beauty in that one person or the gift they have been given and help them to see that gift and beauty in themselves. Life is too short to be mean, rude, selfish, and evil. But for whatever reason, people still choose to be that way. All of us have the choice to be who we want to be at any moment in our life and it doesn't have to be done wearing masks or pretending to be someone else. Just be yourself and love who you were created to be. Unique and beautiful . . . just as you are.

The nucleus of who you are right now is completely dependent on the basis of all the information you have accumulated over the course of your life and what you have then chosen from that information to be attached to your persona and character.

If your mom told you growing up that you were strong, beautiful, and funny, there is a very good chance that you grew up feeling that way and even believe that is who you are now.

One day, a long time ago as a child, I was singing in the kitchen, and my dad overheard me. He yelled from the living room that he thought I had a beautiful singing voice. I will tell you right now, I have never forgot those words. And for some reason, they stuck with me, and I believed him. I have not gone on to a successful singing career, but I have sung many times in church, karaoke, and even at our own

North Bend festival. People seem to enjoy my singing, and I enjoy singing for them. This is the power of our words and our choices.

The same goes for a negative comment or action. Especially if it is a continued barrage of insults and bashing throughout your childhood coming from your parents or guardian. But here is where the power of our choices comes in. You can choose, if you so desire, to ignore and reject those negative insults, and you can change the record that is playing in your head. You are not the result of what someone else thinks or believes you to be. Most of the time, those kinds of rejections are based out of their own insecurities and from the pain of their own past. They are puking on you the negative words and thoughts they inherently believe about themselves. You have the power to change that.

Throughout most of my life, I have struggled to understand who I am and why. I believe this to be a normal step in the process of just plain growing up, but sometimes, people grab ahold of the information that they have been told or have been given about themselves and then choose to believe it. It doesn't have to be that way. *You can change*—if you want to. You can be whoever you want to be, you just have to believe that you can. You can choose to change who you are, a character issue or behavioral issue, something about yourself that you don't particularly like at any time. I have had to do this many times throughout my life.

I try and love all the different people, their walks of life and their stories. I try to be open to the reality that most people are broken and come from some form of brokenness. I don't always succeed in this. My own brokenness will sometimes try and fight back, not allowing me to offer kindness, patience, or compassion to those who are hurting and lashing out.

My initial belief though is that everyone desires and deserves to be loved and accepted. But a lot of people don't believe that they are worthy of love or that they will ever be loved. Everyone has a story to tell, and I will be sharing some of my own stories and my testimony throughout the chapters of this book. I am hoping and praying that this book and my own story will be an inspiration to others. If we choose to shine brightly with the love of Jesus in our hearts, then maybe, just maybe, someone will see that light and ask where it came from.

It is quite remarkable how each of us are learning, growing, and teaching something to ourselves and to somebody else every day of our lives. If you have children, you totally get it. If I even tried to list all that I have learned over the course of my life, it would be endless. I don't know about you, but I am constantly questioning my life, "Why I am here, and what is my purpose?" It seems we are left to our own devices to figure this all out.

I, personally, am a man who loves to see results. When I choose to do something that I believe in, I go after it with all I got. I love seeing the end result of hard work and determination—especially if it is eternally motivated. By storing up treasures in heaven, you are basically filling in the gaps of darkness all around you with light and the love of Jesus. In choosing to move in the direction of love, peace, forgiveness, grace, and mercy, you are choosing to bring light into your world, which can have a tremendous impact to those all around you.

We all can make a choice that can change the lives of thousands of people either in a negative way or in a positive way. One choice can destroy life, and another choice can bring life into this world. We all have to choose what is right and what is wrong and decide what moves people to make choices that can bring life and love or bring death and destruction.

These are questions, I am sure, that have been asked many times throughout our history and even in our own lives. Why, exactly, do people choose to do what they do? What motivates a human being to choose hate, violence, negativity, and evil in their choices? Where does this stem from? What leads them to make these choices? Why does it seem that there is so much sadness, loneliness, and evil in the world? The questions that boggle my mind is where do people get the idea that it is okay to do such horrible and despicable things, evil things to other people? Even worse . . . to innocent children?

I have to ask why? Why did Catholic priests prey on little boys for decades to satisfy their own dark and twisted fantasies? Or coaches and doctors that we trust to take care of our young girls and young women who end up molesting them? Why do men walk into a school and kill innocent children? Why did Hitler have this insatiable desire to wipe out the Jews? Why did the first settlers to America wipe out the Native Americans, their tribes and their culture in the name of God? How could we ever believe that we had the right to make someone else our slave because of the color of their skin? Do we really believe we have been given that right? Where do we get the idea that one race is more important than the other? Aren't we the human race? Don't we all bleed the same color? Don't we all have one beating heart and two lungs to breath? Are we not all from same stock—the race of humans?

How does one come to believe that life has no worth? Where does the disconnect happen in the mind and heart of a human being where they see no reason to live and go so far to even believe that they should become God and end the lives of others?

I have no answers to most of these questions. If I could even try to sum it all up, in my belief and in my opinion, it has been the lack of love and true understanding of how important it is to have God in our lives and to know and understand fully what a real relationship with Jesus looks like. Not religion but a *relationship*.

Let me elaborate here for just a bit. If, throughout history, we integrated into our everyday lives more about the love, truth and forgiveness of Jesus, then there would be more positive changes to personal behaviors and choices that would be made. If they truly knew him, had a relationship with him, truly listened to his words and followed his example, felt his love and forgiveness, and accepted him with faith as their Lord and Savior, a lot of these atrocities and tragedies to mankind would ever take place. Sadly though, we are but sinful man. We will continue to fight against the light of Jesus. Demanding our own way of life, and not the true way!

To those who choose atheism, evolution, agnosticism, and every other form of selfish formulation of life, will continue to make sure that their kind of "faith" will fit into their own objectives and beliefs to satisfy their human desires. Sadly, because of our selfishness, greed, and sin, we will continue as a human race to choose to withhold God from our countries, our schools, and life in general, and we will continue to repeat history.

We cannot change the world until the evil one is vanquished from the earth. He will continue to rule over it and push all the buttons that cause chaos and disbelief in God's only Son. He will continue to win if we let him. You have the freewill to choose what side you want to be on. Choose wisely.

I have made many poor choices in my life that ultimately caused pain to myself and to others. I then allowed my poor choices to consume me with guilt, shame, and remorse. Of course, every one of us will make poor choices in this thing called life. It is what you do after you have made those poor choices, mistakes, or errors that will define you the most. Most people want to hide from their mistakes and pretend they never happened. Sweep them under the rug, lock it up in the closet of your heart, and then hope that it will go away.

Can I just please tell you, in my experience, that never works. In fact, it will end up rotting your soul and devouring your happiness. It will bring separation, anxiety, insecurity, and pain once it surfaces in your relationships and in your life. Give yourself some grace and learn how to forgive yourself, and if needed, ask for forgiveness from the ones you hurt.

It may seem that I have been focusing a lot more on the negative choices that we make in this life and you're right. It seems that the negative or poor choices we make are far more often remembered and have a much greater impact on our lives than do the positive ones. This is why the news is 98 percent negative and 2 percent positive. We almost expect it—like this is normal, which sadly, it can be.

One of my goals in this one beautiful life is to open the eyes and hearts of those who may not have seen what I have seen or heard what I have heard. Our thoughts can deceive us if we let them and even that is a choice we can change. Somehow, if we can just focus in and recognize the power of our choices and change what we don't like, then we can choose wisely!

Anybody who knows me well enough knows that I love '80s music. Some people even tell me that I am stuck in the '80s, which in some form or fashion, is true. Music of the 1980s brought about some of the most creative songs, lyrics, and culture of our time. One song written and sung by one of the most gifted and influential artists of the '80s rings true:

The Man in the Mirror
by Michael Jackson

I'm starting with the man in the mirror
I am asking him to change his ways
And no message could have been any clearer
If you wanna make the world . . . a better place
Take a look at yourself and then make a change.

Life is so very beautiful and full of love. It is really everywhere if you just choose to see it. I have always struggled with the glass half empty or half full concept. To me that is a dull example of how big our world is and all the beauty that is in it. If we could just stop and listen to the birds singing, stop to smell the scents of the flowers and see the beauty in the trees, look up to see the glorious stars, and realize there are beautiful things everywhere! If we could just put our electronics aside more often and look up, not down, there is a beautiful world that we have been given going by each day . . . don't miss it!

If we, as a community, could just for once understand how important loving each other truly is, this world would never be the same. This truth has been taught to me, and I have seen the fruit of its labor. Jesus, the Son of God, came into our world as a human being to open our eyes and help all of us to see that *love* is more powerful than anything else on earth. Probably the most known and repeated verse of the Bible is John 3:16: "For God so loved the world, that He gave His only Son, that whosoever believes in Him should not perish but have eternal life."

Eternal Life. Think about that for a minute. What is eternal life to you? Now that I am almost fifty years old, I have been thinking more and more about this life ending and how much time I might have left. Inevitably, death is a part of life, and none of us can escape this final chapter of our lives. It baffles me each and every time a celebrity that I grew up watching as a child, dies. I am not thinking about dying in a negative way or that I am worried about dying because gratefully, I don't have to. I believe in eternal life and in Jesus Christ, and because of him, we have been given the greatest news we will ever hear in this life!

You and I have been given a choice—a choice to search out and see if this is true or not, or choose to sit by and live our lives ignorantly. We need to ask ourselves, is Jesus real? Is he really the Son of God? Did he really do and say all that he did? Is he really who he says he is? Does he really love me that much that he would die for me? Did he really rise from the dead? The answer to these questions is emphatically *yes*! The verses that follow that most famous of verses, John 3:16, are verses that should also be remembered and put to memory. In John 3:17–21, Jesus says this:

> For God did not send His Son into the world to condemn the world, but in order that the world might be saved through him. Whoever believes in Him is not condemned, but whoever does not believe is condemned already, because he/she has not believed in the name of the only Son of God. And this is the judgement; the light, (Jesus), has come into the world, and people loved the darkness rather than the light because their works were evil. For everyone who does wicked things hates the light and does not come to the light, lest his works should be exposed. But whoever does what is true comes to the light, so that it may be clearly seen that his works have been carried out in God.

If you are like me, you may have asked the question about yourself, "Do I have darkness in me, works of evil, or do I do wicked things?" The truth is, we have all been born into sin. No one, not one person, is sinless in this world except for Jesus. Therefore, what you and I may see as darkness, wickedness, or evil would not seem to calculate into anything that we have done that would fall into this category. Yet, the poor choices we make throughout our lives can very well fall under this category when looked at through the eyes of Jesus.

Selfishness, greed, lust, fornication, adultery, lying, stealing, cheating, etc., these are the sins that we have all committed throughout our lives in one way or another. There are certainly people out there in the world who are very dark, wicked and who do evil things.

I have done things that I am very ashamed of that have fallen under these categories, and they have had an impact on others in a very negative way. In fact, I have made choices throughout my life that are wicked, and they are dark against what is light and what is good. If we choose to turn away from the light, then we are saying we don't need forgiveness, and we want to stay in our darkness and our sin. Again, I don't know about you, but that will *never* be what I would choose or where I want to stay just because of my stubbornness to believe that I don't need saving or that I believe that I am not as bad as the next person!

If we all could just grasp for just one minute the understanding of forgiveness and the amount of love, grace, and mercy that Jesus wants to pour out into everyone, it would change your life like nothing else on this earth.

Our choices are always right in front of us. We are all born into this world. We live our lives, and in the process, we have to choose to either accept the free gift of eternal life or choose death. Let me ask you a question. If someone pulled a loaded gun on you and pointed it squarely at your head, would you cry and plea for mercy? Would you want to live more than anything else? Would you cry out to God for help? To save you? It amazes me that people every day choose to live as if there really is no God. No creator. No one behind all of our existence. No intelligent designer.

The human body is the most intricate piece of machinery in the world with thousands of parts all working together as one. The discoveries of the human body continue to baffle and amaze doctors and scientists, and they still don't know how some things work. With everything we know about life, this earth, our galaxy, and our bodies, and a lot of people still don't want to admit that there is an intelligent designer who made all of this with finite precision and detail.

Even the most skeptic of people cry out to God to save them when life is on the edge of death. When it comes down to the final act of their life, that is when they choose to reach out for God, just in case he might be real. I have had many times throughout my life where friends of mine who don't believe in God ask me to pray for them or a loved one who has suddenly become very sick or injured in an accident. Why do we wait and only decide then, when it is absolutely necessary, that we need God or hope he will save us or cure someone who is very sick or dying? Why wait till the end? I don't want to wait until the end. I want to know now! And what if, you or I have no opportunity or time left to say yes to Jesus at our last breath?

All of us only get so many chances. The choice is ours. God is certainly not a tyrant forcing his love or his will on us. But the love I know and have experienced is nothing short of miraculous. And that is the love of his Son, Jesus. He became the beacon of light and love to all who have been searching to help us understand this thing called life. This is where, I believe, lies the most important choice of all. To believe or not to believe, that is the question. We choose to live and do according to what we believe.

If we only choose to see one color of a rainbow, then we have already crippled our hearts and minds to consider that there would even be more colors than just the one. I have always believed that what you put into your mind and heart is what will eventually be expressed out of the existence of your life—light or darkness, gratitude or greed, love or hate. Garbage in will become garbage that comes out. If you only listen to music that is full of negative, violent, or evil subject matter, then there is a good chance that your life will have those types of temperaments and behaviors added into it.

When parents raise their children to believe in racism, live it and breathe it, this is all they know. It becomes a part of their very existence. It has been ingrained into their heart and mind and they can't see or feel anything else. They only see the hatred and racism for that particular color and believe they are inferior. They are brainwashed into believing that everyone else is less than and that one color is greater than another. Color blind is what they truly become.

Somehow, we have to open the door to our minds and the windows to our hearts so we can help each other to see that there are many more colors to the rainbow than just one. How is it that it is so incredibly difficult to see, from a generally coherent human being, that we are all the same? We all have two eyes, two ears, two arms and legs with feet, and hands attached to them. If we could only see the world as little children do, then there would be no racism, no hatred, no killing, and no judgment—only *love*. But that is not the world we live in, and it is killing us.

Something happens to us on the journey from child-like love to becoming adults. Somewhere along the way, we feel we have the right to judge someone by the way they look, the way they walk, the color of their skin, and the way they talk. We don't know their story, and they don't know ours. Why begin to believe that we know who they are or what they have been through by our first glance? Have we put on their shoes and walked where they have walked?

I have often struggled, as I know many of you have, with regard to giving money to panhandlers and to the poor. I often worry it will not go to supply them with the necessary nutrients that their body needs but will end up going to drugs and alcohol. It seems that this demographic is growing. My wife and I have had the beautiful opportunity to serve those who are homeless. All I can say is, don't ever judge a book by its cover. I have had grown men hugging me and crying on my shoulder just because someone took the time to show them they are not forgotten and that they are important and loved right where they are. Not all of them are struggling with addictions. A lot of them are there because of abandonment, loneliness, abuse, poor choices, and mental illness. We are free to choose to love instead of ignore. In Jesus's day, he made it his message, his mission, by doing and showing his love to every walk of life. But, he especially had a soft place in his heart for those who were outcasts and the lowest of the lows.

> Then the King will say to those on his right, "Come, you who are blessed by my Father, inherit the Kingdom prepared for you from the creation of the world. For I was hungry, and you fed me. I was thirsty and you gave me a drink, I was a stranger, and you invited me into your home. I was naked and you gave me clothing. I was sick, and you cared for me. I was in prison, and you visited me." Then the righteous ones will reply, "Lord, when did we ever see you hungry and feed you? Or thirsty and give you something to drink? Or a stranger and show you hospitality? Or naked and give you clothing? When did we ever see you sick or in prison and visit you?" And the King will say, "I tell you the truth, when you did it to one of the least of these my brothers and sisters, you were doing it to me!" (Matt. 25:34–40)

If you know who Jesus is or if you ever decide that you really want to know who Jesus was and still is, this is him! He longs to wrap his arms around each and every one of us, and tell us it is going to be okay. His love has brought me to my knees sobbing uncontrollably many times throughout my life. His forgiveness of my life, my sins, and my choices has simply blown me away. I am in awe of him whose love never ends. Even while nailed to cross beams with nails as long as my foot, and beaten and slashed through the skin and flesh to the bone and a woven crown of thorns on his head, he still loved and forgave those who were mocking, persecuting, and killing him. It is his love and forgiveness—his story—that compels me to choose to be more like him every day.

In the Gospel of Luke, Jesus says this while being crucified on the cross: "Father, forgive them, for they know not what they are doing" (Luke 23:34).

What is the meaning of this phrase, "Forgive them, for they know not what they are doing?" Jesus's words from the cross asked God the Father to forgive those who were putting him to death. More widely, of course, was Jesus's plea for all of humanity? "Forgive them all, for they are lost and hurting."

I have worked hard to instill in my children the importance of seeing everyone as equal. We are no better than anyone else. Love and respect everyone the same and be the one who stands up for the one who cannot stand up for themselves. Be the voice for those who have no voice. Help everyone in need if possible. Serve others with the love of Jesus. Find your purpose in this life and seek out the gifts you have been given so that your Heavenly Father will be glorified. Learn what forgiveness is and how to recognize when you are wrong and ask for forgiveness.

Choose wisely in this life, and love . . . with a love that is without reserve or on condition of this or that. Do not give to others with an expectation of getting something in return.

In Romans 5:6–11, Paul says:

> For while we were still weak, at the right time Jesus died for the ungodly. For one will scarcely die for a righteous person—though perhaps for a good person one would dare even to die—but God shows His love for us in that while we were still sinners, Christ died for us. Since, therefore, we have now been justified by his blood, much more shall we be saved by him from the wrath of God. For if while we were still enemies we were reconciled to God by the death of his Son, much more, now that we are reconciled, shall we be saved by his life!

You may think or believe that this life is all about you, I learned years ago that it is *not*. It's not about you or me, it's all about Jesus. This life you have been given is such a beautiful gift. He wants so badly for us to turn to him so he can love us even more. He wants to heal us and give us freedom from the diseases of this world, the addictions, the darkness and the pain, the guilt and shame that we created from our own choices. If we would just choose to seek him out and lay our sin at his feet.

We all have been given this opportunity, our own freewill to look for him. Most of us are given ample time and endless opportunities to find God. A lot of us don't choose wisely to find him. We live in a world full of information at our fingertips, more so than any other time in history, yet we choose to be ignorant to the truth.

> Can anything ever separate us from Christ's love? Does it mean he no longer loves us if we have trouble or calamity, or are persecuted, or hungry, or destitute, or in danger, or threatened with death? No, despite all these things, overwhelming victory is ours through Christ, who loved us. And I am convinced that nothing can ever separate us from God's love. Neither death nor life, neither angels nor demons, neither our fears for today nor our worries about tomorrow—not even the powers of hell can separate us from God's love. No power in the sky above or in the earth below—indeed, nothing in all creation will ever be able to separate us from the love of God that is revealed in Christ Jesus our Lord. (Rom. 8:35–39)

We are all broken, and we all fall short of earning or even deserving God's unconditional love. I struggled with this one concept for far too long in this life. Not believing that I, a sinner, who struggled with sexual sin, deserved to be forgiven for my inability to stay clean and sinless. This was a lie of course. God's love *is* unconditional. When Jesus hung on that cross, he hung there for all your sins! Not just for today's or yesterday's sins—*all* of your sins. Yesterday, today, and tomorrow!

I was set free from my sexual addiction because of Jesus. His love, mercy, grace, and truth from some very close friends helped me to get where I am now, today. That doesn't mean it is gone and will never be an issue again. What it means is, is that I am in recovery, and it no longer has its grip on me. I no longer struggle with that sin in my life. Jesus helped me to break those chains of bondage and now, I can rejoice about my victories in Christ.

One of the most important factors that people sometimes miss in the beautiful creation of God's church is community. I have personally seen and experienced the greatest amount of time and love given from one person to another through friendship, community, fellowship, worship, love, and support of those who choose to be there for others in their addictions, hang-ups, and hardships. James 5:16 says it best: "Confess your sins to each other and pray for each other so that you may be healed. The earnest prayer of a righteous person has great power and produces wonderful results."

When we truly understand the importance of togetherness, support, love, and patience for each other, we begin to understand what it means to be Jesus to each other. We begin to see the sin, not the sinner. Which brings about compassion, love, and acceptance. We long to see them recover from the pain and wounds of their past, which will hopefully lead to recovery from their personal addictions.

When I read and understood years ago what Romans 8:1 *really* meant, it hit me like a brick to the face. Paul says in Romans 8:1: "There is therefore now *no condemnation* for those that are in Christ Jesus."

You are no longer condemned for the sins you have committed, neither yesterday, today, or tomorrow when you accept Jesus into your heart and into your life! We have been set free from sin and death. No more shall we have to fear death or condemnation because of the love of this one man, Jesus, the Son of God. He took upon himself the sin of the *whole world* so that we may live—the one true sacrifice. If you can fathom this truth and understand its eternal ramifications, then you will understand the depth of its importance in your life right now. If you haven't already accepted this free gift from the one who created you, may I suggest you think about it and come to your own conclusion?

I know the importance of this one choice and the good news that comes with it. It is a choice of surrender and sacrifice. It is a choice of unselfishness and humility. But it is also a choice of love and generosity, freedom, forgiveness, mercy, and grace. I choose light and love as my path to take in this world. It is a choice that I have chosen wisely because of the hope I have in me and because I know, one day, I will see Jesus face to face.

"We ask God to give you complete knowledge of his will and to give you spiritual wisdom and understanding. Then the way you live will always honor and please the Lord, and your lives will produce every kind of good fruit. All the while, you will grow as you learn to know God better and better" (Col. 1:9–1).

CHAPTER 2

FREEDOM OF FORGIVENESS

Don't worry about anything; instead, pray about everything.
Tell God what you need, and thank him for all he has
done. Then you will experience God's peace, which
exceeds anything we can understand. His peace will guard
your hearts and minds as you live in Christ Jesus.
—Philippians 4:6–7

Get rid of all bitterness, rage, anger, harsh words and
slander, along with every form of malice. Instead, be
kind and compassionate to one another, forgiving one
another, just as God through Christ has forgiven you.
—Ephesians 4:31–32

W hen I was in my teens, I made choices mainly based on if it was
going to be fun, dangerous, or simply crazy. I lived every day with
a sense of purpose, and that purpose was to entertain people and
hopefully make them laugh. If possible, I wanted to bring joy and
laughter into the lives of those around me so we all could forget for a
moment the struggles of our lives. I also loved the sense of adventure,
the attention, the challenge, and the shock factor. I would jump off
every bridge I could find and take chances at every turn.

Needless to say, there were many times where I probably didn't choose so wisely. But the one thing I did love about those years is that I lived them with passion and a sense of urgency. I didn't care what others thought about me, and I did what I did without regret. I haven't entirely changed from then, I still live life with passion and intensity. I look back now and believe that I thoroughly enjoyed my teenage years and somehow knew that they wouldn't last very long.

I chose to make amazing memories that were unforgettable, adventurous, fun, and crazy that I could look back on with joy and laughter. I hope I brought some of those same things to others who happened to be in my life at that time.

When adulthood came calling at the very young age of twenty-one, I was definitely not ready. I was basically twenty-one going on sixteen. I had just moved to Hawaii with my girlfriend two weeks prior and was just about to start a new job when *pow* . . . guess who's going to be a father? Choices, they always come back to show us the reality and the truth of our actions. You will always reap what you sow.

At this time of my life, marriage and fatherhood were the farthest thing from my mind. I wasn't done living dangerously. I wasn't done being crazy, but here I was, sitting on a beach in Waikiki, asking myself, what have I done and what the heck do I do now? I know now . . . I lived a little too carelessly and dangerously.

Our choices can set us on a path we never knew existed or if chosen wisely, they can set us on a path, which determines our focus and passion. Sometimes, what you want in life is not inevitably what you get. I was blessed with a beautiful baby boy, my son, Dalton, from a choice that I made that had a *huge* impact on my life, and he has been one of my greatest joys. The marriage didn't last, but my son gave me purpose, direction, and the courage to heal, change, and grow. I will admit that I wasn't the greatest dad. I failed miserably many times, but I never stopped trying to be the best dad that I could be. If I failed, I asked for forgiveness, and I changed what I could for the better.

My son is now twenty-six and getting married in three months. He is getting ready to begin his own family and is already making wise choices. I look forward to seeing my son and his wife live their lives and choose what their priorities will be in their marriage. There really is no marriage or life handbook out there that is going to help you or give you the proper direction for your life. Most of the time, we all are just wingin' it! We hope that this choice or that choice is the right one. At least that was the way it was for me.

I am hopeful that my son and his wife will have a much more solid foundation in which to stand on and begin this chapter of their lives. I, on the other hand, was not so fortunate.

My childhood, like many others, was filled with many broken roads, abuse, and unhealthy circumstances. Navigating out of my situation was a miracle in itself. And by the grace of God and his direction, I was able to choose to make something that was dark and full of sadness and abandonment into something beautiful, in the only way God knows how.

I like the saying I heard from another one of my favorite movies, *the Shawshank Redemption*, "Either you get busy living or you get busy dying." Through all of my tears, frustration, sadness, and loneliness as a child and even into my adult life, I knew there had to be something beautiful that would or could be manifest out of the madness of my life that I had been exposed to. It was up to me and my choices as to how it would unfold. I chose to get busy living.

I had been brought up in the church for most of my childhood, which was my saving grace. I went to Sunday school, Bible camp, and then eventually Youth Group for most of my young life and have always believed that there is light and love in this world even when I wasn't experiencing it personally as a child. I longed to understand who this man, Jesus, truly was.

I remember being glued to the TV when around Easter time, one of the major channels would play the six-hour miniseries, *Jesus of Nazareth*. I loved watching it every time it came on. Why did he choose to purposefully die on a cross for us—all of us, and to die in the most tortuous way? He made the choice for us. A choice that would turn the world on its head and make us question all that surrounds us.

We choose a thousand times over how we see and feel, think and react, speak and listen. We are all searching for answers to our existence that helps us make sense of everything. Some of us though, are carefully choosing to find only what fits their own belief system. Right or wrong, guided or misguided. From our experiences, our teaching, our upbringing, from death and life, from movies, books, all forms of media and the daily news. All of these different sources around us break into our lives, our reality and have an impact on what we choose to believe.

It amazes me to what degree the things of this world impact my life. Something that is so precious and yet so delicate can be manipulated with just a single word, an act, or even a song. One simple act of kindness can change a life and has even helped some people to choose life over suicide. You never know what your actions or words will do for someone at that very moment of their day.

Do you love the person you are seeing in the mirror? Not in a vain way, but do you love *you*? Do you believe you have been a good person? Do you believe people really like you for you? Are you a good dad, mother, husband, or wife? Are you a good friend? Are you loved? Do you feel that you are important? Will anyone miss you when your time here on earth comes to an end? If you died, who would really come to your funeral, and what would they really say about the person you have chosen to become? Did you love enough, give enough, or care enough? What does it all mean? What is this life really all about?

What you choose to make of your life, will define who you think you are, in every category of your life. The mind is a powerful tool, but the heart is the foundation of your soul. Listen to the wisdom and love of Jesus in his words from Matthew 6:19–21: "Do not store up for yourselves treasure on earth, where moths eat them and rust destroy them, and where thieves break in and steal. Store your treasures in heaven where moths can't eat, rust cannot destroy and thieves do not break in and steal. For wherever your treasure is, there will your heart be also."

When I read these words for the first time, the love and the truth that is in them just blew me away. When I fully understood these words, I knew I would be impacted from that day on by the truths that were within them. Most of what Jesus taught and did goes against the grain of all that the world preaches of what is most important in this life. The treasure you love will become the treasure you live for and are passionate about. Your life, your time, and your money will revolve around what you feel is your treasure. And, like it says, wherever your treasure is, there is where your heart lies. I believe it is incredibly important to evaluate what your treasure is and if it is for eternal purposes or selfish ones. Your life, your soul, literally sits on the ledge of this truth. Don't be foolish or ignorant to see the value in the words of Jesus and to follow them. You cannot serve God and money. There is no such thing as a profitable gospel.

I have learned that when you give to someone in need without any selfish motive and never expecting anything in return, it is simply the greatest feeling in the world. When you look into the eyes of someone who is so desperate, in so much need, and you are able to meet that need, purely, with no other purpose but love for that person, that is when you have entered into the *Twilight Zone* of love and humanity. That is where God dwells and that is where Jesus works. I have been there many times with tears flowing down my cheeks uncontrollably, my heart overflowing and tugging me left and right—a piercing of my soul so deep that I will never be the same. This is where I long to be. A choice I hope everyone chooses to make in their life. The choice to make a difference.

I only want to fill my life with memories of the treasures I was able to experience in choosing to make a difference in someone else's life and for God's kingdom. I can only hope that God will allow me to continue to bring him glory. In all my days on this earth, this is what I truly believe life is all about. Loving others deeply and unselfishly and loving God passionately.

I too, have believed the lies of this world. I, too, have fallen for things that the world says is important. I, too, have chosen sex over a godly life, possessions over choosing to help others instead. It is a never-ending battle to choose what is right, what is pure and to choose love. And I too, have beat myself up or until I was black and blue for the choices I had made in my life. But that is not my story or even your story. That is just a part of our story. You can choose to rewrite your story at any time of your life.

You can choose, like I have had to do many times, to forgive yourself for those horrible choices and ask forgiveness of those you hurt along the way. You can choose to stop beating yourself up and learn how to forgive yourself and love yourself again. Asking for forgiveness is the first huge step into this healing process. Asking for forgiveness is one of the hardest things you will ever do, but the most rewarding. Giving forgiveness to those who hurt you is also very difficult but absolutely necessary.

Reconciliation is extremely beautiful. It has to start with you though. Only *you* can change your surroundings. Only *you* can choose to change what has been done—the wrong that has been committed. It is up to you to start the healing process, and forgiveness is the key to the locked door. Guess what? You're human; you made a mistake. Build a bridge and get over it. Get mad like I did and make a choice to change.

This is what is so beautiful about God's amazing grace. All you have to do is to make a choice to be done with whatever you don't like about who you are and start making the necessary changes to make sure you are successful going forward. Delete everything that is unhealthy in your life. And I mean *delete* all of your "so called" friends, girlfriends, boyfriends, behaviors, unhealthy places, material things, unhealthy habits, social media, and false relationships. Everything you need to vanquish from your life so that a new chapter can begin. Delete it all. This is an extremely important part of the process of becoming healthy, happy, and on your way to finding joy in your life.

Allow God to heal you and let his forgiveness shine down over you like the most cleansing shower you have ever taken washing away all the dirt, shame, sin, and guilt. Don't worry, God already knows what you look like naked, and he already knows all that you have done. He truly loves you right where you are. Trust me, I have had to do this several times throughout my life. It is a revamping of your surroundings and your life, like putting on new skin. This is what the Bible calls the renewing of your mind. In a way, you are starting over. You have hit the replay button and are recording over it a new way of life.

When I completely gave my life over to Christ, I needed to know that from all that I have been given, all that I experienced, and all that I had suffered had a reason and a purpose.

Why do we cry when seeing great triumph in the lives of people who have come back from almost unbeatable odds? We cry because we love to see the underdog come out of nowhere and win in this thing called life. We love to see injustice ratified. We love to see people conquer their fears and succeed. We love to see good people doing good things for those who were in great need of their love. We love to see people who were once suffering, given a second chance at life. We love to see redemption and forgiveness to what otherwise was a destructive and broken relationship. We love to see people who love on other people for no other reason than the purest reason of all—*love*.

I took my daughter, Trinity, on a daddy-daughter date to see the new movie, I *Can Only Imagine,* based on the true life story of Bart Millard, the lead singer of my all-time favorite Christian group, MercyMe. It is the story behind how this song of the same name came to be created. It was absolutely incredible. I had no idea how tragic and sad his life had been growing up with such an abusive father. But what came out of it and the beauty that God had used from it was nothing short of a miracle. At the end of the movie, as I sat there sobbing uncontrollably, I realized that many parts of his life resembled mine—the pain, the abuse, the loneliness, and the abandonment. Suffering to understand why we had to experience all that we had to. We both had to lean on music and especially God to survive through the torment of our childhood.

Hello, my name is Don, and I am a crier. I am, and have become, an extremely emotional creature, and I believe God has taken my experiences as a child and helped me to be more empathetic and sensitive to others and their pain, their suffering, and the very lives, which they live.

I have been searching to know and understand why we have to suffer and experience pain or why we choose to cause it. I wanted to know how to ask for forgiveness to those I have hurt and how to move past it, how do I forgive someone and move on? Or do I have to carry it with me wherever I go for the rest of my life? I cry because I feel others' pain and suffering, and I want to help them, hug them, and love them.

I used to sit in the front window of our house in Seattle when I was five years old, watching and waiting, wondering when my mom would come home. She never did. And, sadly, for most of my childhood, she struggled financially to be able to see us boys and spend good quality time with us.

When I was four or five years old, my mom chose to leave us kids, my two older brothers and me, and divorce our father. She brought us into this world, and then she chose to leave us behind and impact our lives in a very negative way. Please understand though, I have forgiven my mom, and I have had to work very hard at doing just that. I have experienced tremendous pain and suffering because of her decision and the decisions my dad chose to make because of it. But, I now know that even through tremendous suffering, something can blossom and grow into an amazing story of triumph, forgiveness, love, and truth.

My mom loved us deeply, but she was still carrying the baggage of her own childhood and the pain and suffering of her parents' choices and actions. Which, sadly, spilled into our lives as children like a generational curse. And, my dad, well, he was struggling, too. After the divorce from my mom, my dad carried with him the baggage of failure, loneliness, and hopelessness, and it became an ultimate train wreck for us all.

After my mom left, I can recall a time or two when my dad would crawl into my bed, snuggle me, and just cry. He was now alone, left behind, and left with the responsibility of raising his three young boys. Even though his choices ended up hurting us even more, I know he did his best, and he loved us.

Here again lies the truth of our actions and choices. With every choice, good or bad, positive or negative, there will be a cause and effect from that choice—a reaction to the action. Forgiveness once again had to be called upon to drain away the pain of those choices. The power of forgiveness is unimaginable while you are overpowered by your hate, anger, distrust, and disgust in the person with whom you do not want to forgive. But the power of that forgiveness will set you on a course of love, trust, reconciliation, and hopefully healthier relationships.

My story is one of healing from that very power. Quite honestly, I never wanted to forgive those who caused me pain. I wanted them to see my suffering, see my pain, and feel horrible about it—remorseful if possible. I believed they didn't earn such a reward as forgiveness or that I should be the one to give it to them. But that was a huge lie.

In reality, when we choose to forgive those that hurt us, we are actually giving back to ourselves the freedom that is so necessary for happiness and love, it is like air to our lungs when we are suffocating. We are also setting the accused free from the pain of their poor choices.

There is no greater freedom you can give to yourself when you choose to release someone who has hurt you so that you can truly live. Even the opposite is just as powerful, when you choose to ask for forgiveness from someone you wronged or hurt. Forgiveness comes from within, deep in your soul, for there lies the power for freedom.

Jesus's choice to endure great suffering because of his love for us is a concept that many truly don't understand. And this even becomes a stumbling block to their faith and the understanding of how much power is in the act of forgiveness. I have spent my entire life seeking to understand this and many other things that are wrapped up in this man, Jesus. I believe without a doubt that he truly is the Son of God. With all my studies, all the books I have read, all the stories I have heard and things I have seen, through my pain and recovery, through my journey and my own experiences in this life and the love I have felt deep within me over and over again, I cannot and will not come to any other conclusion. But it always comes down to a choice.

Not long after my mom left when I was five years old, my dad, my brothers, and I moved from Seattle to Everett. My dad then hired a woman named Betty who was chosen to be our live-in nanny. She was sweet at first, offering love and affection, which had been missing in our lives since our mom decided to divorce our dad. I believe this is what my dad found intriguing along with the fact that she was sixteen years younger than he was. Shortly after this, my dad married Betty, and she forever changed the course of our lives.

My dad made the choice to marry Betty to help solve some personal issues he was dealing with such as loneliness, failure of his first marriage, and to seal a deal to solve the problem of someone watching over us boys. Right out of the gate, she got pregnant with my younger brother, Buck. A short time later, while pregnant, is when the real Betty started to appear. She became very violent and acted out with anger at the drop of a hat. She was very strict and hard on us kids, demanding we live by her directives, ideals, standards, and her religious legalism. I can still see the rage and evil in her eyes.

She was brought up very poor and lived on a farm in Eastern Washington, the youngest of eight children, and her father was very strict. She had dropped out of high school around the ninth or tenth grade because of a car accident that left her in a full body cast for months. She never recovered well from that occurrence. I remember her telling me that she had felt she had lost her childhood from that experience.

One of the many things that burned me up inside was to watch how my dad would wait on her hand and foot. She would literally ring a bell from her bedside table when she needed or wanted something from my dad. I finally asked my dad, "Why do you wait on her like that?" And he told me, "I would rather she be in the bedroom and away from us than to be out here with us." If that doesn't give you a glimpse of the challenge of this woman, I don't know what will. She continued to become an absolute horror of a woman and abused us mentally, emotionally, spiritually, and even physically.

Sadly, my dad was born without much of spine (metaphorically), and that became an even bigger problem for us boys. He never stood up for us when Betty would be out of control for no apparent reason, screaming and swearing at us, throwing things or using a wooden paddle on us that she painted a face on and chose to call,

"Mr. Persuasion." All of this killed me internally, and then my dad chose to give her all the power of parenting and disciplining us. I needed him more than ever, and he chose to not be there for me or my brothers. The choices he made left me hurting, bitter, and extremely angry. With my mom having already abandoned us, now I felt abandoned from my dad, as well.

So here lies the foundation of my story—an extremely painful struggle and even more painful past of abandonment, abuse, hopelessness, and a lack of love. I believe my dad loved us, but he was horrible at showing us. My mom loved us but lacked the ability to give it to us. I even believe that Betty loved us to a point but was too consumed with the pain of her own past and the struggles of life that she just couldn't get over it. So, my brothers and I had only each other to lean on. We grabbed ahold of Jesus and each other to survive.

When I was sixteen years old, I ran away from that home because of the abuse, the non-existent support of my dad, and the unhealthy conditions that I had been exposed to for eleven long years, I was finally done. I was done being treated like a slave, being ignored by a dad who just didn't seem to care and in a home where I didn't feel loved. I went to live with my older brother, Dave, and his wife, Mary, who graciously opened their home to me. My mom finally decided to move out to North Bend because of my desperate situation, and also because I had cried and pleaded with her that I needed her here with me. Around six months later, my mom arrived and so began a new chapter in relationship, forgiveness, and love.

Years after leaving us kids, the one person that ended up showing me with her own actions and choices what the true healing powers of forgiveness can bring, was my very own mom. As I finally got the opportunity to start to know and understand my mom and her story of her own childhood, it started to make sense to me as to how and why she made the choices she did with regard to us boys and my dad. In many ways, she was reenacting her own childhood, but this time, she was the mom and not the child.

As more time grew and her story became more and more apparent to me, I couldn't help but be baffled and amazed as to how she could forgive what had been done to her. Alcoholism had abused her and her three brothers through the likeness of her father and mother. Her mom ended up leaving because her dad was physically abusing her. Now, their dad couldn't take care of them while living in Oregon, so my mom took over caring for herself and her three brothers until eventually the state came for them and took them out of their home and away from their father. Foster home after foster home, abuse and the separation of her siblings took its toll on them.

My mom was the oldest and felt the overwhelming responsibility of keeping them safe and together. This of course would bring about the horrible circumstances that they would have to endure as young children trying to understand the choices and actions that their own parents brought onto them. My mom never did verbalize the great detail of the suffering she and her brothers experienced at the hands of strangers, but I know it was a lot.

But even in all of this suffering, immense pain, abandonment, and abuse, she forgave her parents and those strangers who had hurt her and her brothers. She had shown me a deep sense of forgiveness that was so real and unimaginable. How can you forgive them, your mom and dad, all those abusive people, the poor choices and utter loss of love, innocence, and tenderness? How can you forgive them? How?

Through her eyes, which are the windows to her soul, I could see the love growing there, which should have been filled with anger, resentment, and bitterness. But, instead, she chose forgiveness and love. This was my first real understanding of the truth and the power of forgiveness.

Her brothers, by the way, did not handle very well the life they had been given. They carried the pain, hurt, anger, and abuse that they suffered with from their parents and those strangers into their own lives. The result of their parents' choices affected them and their relationships greatly. The only cousins I knew from my mom's side suffered greatly at the hands of their father who abused them and their mother.

Life has a way of continuing this generational abuse. People who have been extremely hurt and have experienced tremendous abuse as children unfortunately end up doing the same thing to their own families, to their own kids. This generational curse can be stopped. It can end with whoever chooses to recognize their pain, the truth of their actions, and decide to stop the madness and the cycle of abuse. It has to start with the power of forgiveness.

True forgiveness of one's self is attainable. The love and forgiveness of Jesus Christ is where it all begins. Then the journey to forgiveness of those who abused you can begin. Choose to break free from the chains of bondage over you with the power of forgiveness.

As I have told you clearly in the true stories of my childhood, I hated Betty with a passion that burned very intense and bright. Being that I was young and that I had accepted Christ into my heart, this was a challenge for me to look past, and though I knew that it was wrong to hate her, I couldn't seem to find the compassion to make that happen. Eleven years of her hell and wickedness was buried deep inside me and right beside that was my anger and frustration with my dad and mom. And there, that day, looking into my mom's eyes, I began to understand what forgiveness is. This was the beginning of my journey.

For me to understand the power of this forgiveness, I first needed to understand where its power truly came from. For me to truly understand the source of forgiveness was to go to the very source itself, Jesus of Nazareth. No one else on this earth and in the history of humanity has shown more love, mercy, and forgiveness as Jesus did on that cross and continues to do so today.

After I had accepted Christ into my heart when I was eight years old, I called my mom and told her that I wanted her to also accept Jesus into her heart. I told her that I didn't want to go to heaven without her and that I wanted to see her there. Telling my mom this was the breaking point for her. She cried and told me that, what I had said to her that day was the beginning of her journey to invite Jesus into her heart. Today, my mom has one of the strongest faiths I have ever seen.

Throughout my childhood, one of my biggest challenges to all of this, and in my relationship with God, was the person who brought me to Christ. Ironically, the person who introduced me to Jesus came from the most unlikely source and from the person I despised the most in my life, my step-mom, Betty.

The one person who did *not* exemplify Jesus in any way was the one who introduced me to him. Sadly, I struggled to understand who Jesus truly was because of the example that Betty was showing us through her religion and legalism, instead of having an intimate relationship with him. I also struggled to understand why someone who was supposed to love and cherish us kids was abusing us in so many ways. I was trying to understand why I was hurting so much if he loves me so much.

Please don't be misled. God works in the most amazing ways and makes something beautiful out of even the most wretched of circumstances. God's love and light show up in even the darkest of places. I didn't want to accept that this was one of those places.

"He makes all things beautiful in its time" (Eccles. 3:11).

As a child, I would stand in front of the bathroom mirror full of absolute rage just screaming silently to myself with tears falling off my cheeks. Again and again, I would ask, "Why, God? Why do I have to put up with this?" God would inevitably bring something beautiful out of a horrendous situation. And my story is only one of thousands I have heard of that involve redemption, recovery and resolve at the hands and feet of Jesus Christ. He is the great healer and lover of our souls. He brings salvation, love, friendship, and mercy to a hurting and dying world. Forgiveness is what I needed, and Jesus showed that to me time and time again. And through my pain and suffering I learned what it meant to forgive.

My mom showed me what it means and how it can change your life. She told me that if I chose not to forgive, then I would carry all that anger and pain like a ball and chain around with me for the rest of my life. And if you choose to do the same, then the ones that hurt you will continue to win and continue to hurt you and then in turn, you could potentially end up hurting someone else.

Hurt people . . . hurt people. Break the chains that God broke for you. Forgive those that hurt you just like Jesus forgave you for all you needed to be forgiven for. That was the most important and deepest truth that I needed to hear in this life. It started with the woman I despised and ended with the one I needed the most.

All in all, I am the man I am because of the challenges, the suffering, and the pain of my life. Through all that suffering and pain, forgiveness and love, I am that much more compassionate and loving. I cry for those who are hurting and long to give them rest from the burdens they have been carrying all these years.

God's love overwhelmed me to the deepest core of my soul and being. He touched my heart so deeply and lovingly that I seriously had no choice but to love with a love overflowing. And so it is, to choose to love and to forgive and to ask for forgiveness has been the greatest choice I could have ever made for my life. It has literally changed my life in so many ways, I will probably never know what they all are. But I do know this, the choice to change and make it better either by love, forgiveness, passion, or truth, is a choice worth making and a choice you will never regret.

Years later, I ended up forgiving Betty for all she put us through, but it would take years of repetitively forgiving her over and over again until eventually one day, it was done, and it was gone. Over time and with persistence, my forgiveness for her finally won. Forgiveness became a shining light in my soul, and in my heart, I was healed. Forgiveness had won the battle, and I was set free from the war. You will never forget what was done to you—but even that will start to fall away after the healing has taken place. Choose to forgive everyone who has hurt you and genuinely ask for forgiveness from the ones you have hurt. That is where you will eventually find your true freedom.

CHAPTER 3

WHAT IS YOUR MILK?

Be on the alert, stand firm in the faith, act like men
and be strong. Let all that you do be done in love.
—1 Corinthians 16:13–14

We are all desperate, and that is in fact the only state
appropriate to a human being who wants to know God.
Having fallen from the absolute ideal, we have nowhere
to land but in the safety net of absolute grace.
—Philip Yancey, "The Jesus I Never Knew"

"Cinderella Man" is a nickname that was given to a heavyweight boxing champion by the name of James J. Braddock during the time of the Great Depression in the 1930s. His true-life story was made into a movie in 2005 starring Russell Crowe and directed by Ron Howard. This story is an amazing example of survival and determination when your back is against the wall and your family is desperate for the very basic needs of life.

James Braddock was an Irish-American boxer from New Jersey and former light heavyweight contender, who was forced to give up boxing after breaking his hand in the ring. This becomes a great burden to his wife and three young kids as he now does not have an income to bring in to take care of his family.

During the Great Depression, Braddock has to try and pick up any manual labor where he can as a longshoreman to support his family, even with his injured hand. Unfortunately, he struggles to get work each day, and they end up losing everything they own. Eventually, things get so bad that there is no food to eat, and they can't even pay for a bottle of milk from the milkman. The power gets shut off, and his son eventually steals food from the local market to feed his brother and sister. This brings great distress to Braddock and his wife as they see their children get worse and become sick from malnutrition and the lack of heat in their home.

Braddock promised his oldest son that he and his siblings would never be sent away because of the conditions of their lives and the lack thereof. After all of their loss and the power being shut off, the kids' sickness was getting worse, and the mother, played by Rene Zellweger, couldn't take it anymore and chose to go against Braddock's refusal to send them away.

She sent the kids to her sister's home, and when Braddock came home from work that day and found them gone, he was furious. He had no other choice than to go back to the place where all the boxing managers and producers hung out and begged for money, so he could get his kids back. Not long after this, his luck changed, and he was offered another chance at boxing. This time, his hand was healed and his opportunity to make something of himself was fueled by his determination to provide for his family.

After he won that fight, he continued to win and eventually became the heavyweight champion of the world. At a prefight interview, the reporters asked him about his inspiration to come back so strong and win so fiercely. His answer was simple. "Milk." "Milk?" they asked, "Yes, Milk."

I have never forgot that movie and the incredible message it tells. Of course, it made me cry because that is what I do in movies that touch my heart so deeply. I have often asked myself, "What is my milk? What sets me afire to do something radical and with a tenacity that nothing will stop me?"

Around twenty years ago, I ended a ten–year management career with QFC and moved into a "salesman career" as a route driver for Hostess-Wonder bread company. It was a bold move as I had needed a drastic change from what I had been doing for so long, and it all began with a major mistake I had made.

About a year before I left QFC, I was moving up the ranks in management and feeling confident about my career choice. I had just been promoted into a third position assistant store manager at Rainier Beach QFC, and I felt accomplished and successful. I was progressing through the management ranks feeling pretty cocky and good about myself. Little did I know that the grocery world would soon come crashing down around me.

It was in the evening around 6:00–7:00 p.m., and the store was hopping. I was the manager in charge that evening, and I had just jumped into the check stand to relieve a checker who needed a break. As busy as we were, I was moving pretty fast in the checkout line to try and move the customers along as quickly as possible. Now, around this time, the Tobacco and Alcohol Enforcement Team of Washington State was on a mission to stop underage drinking, and they were doing it with a passion.

Barely looking up from my check stand to say "Hi" and grabbing the next customer in line, I instantly started scanning their items so they would feel I was trying to move them along as rapidly as possible. What I failed to do was to take the time to really look at who I was helping. I looked up rapidly, said, "Hi, how are you?" and then proceeded to scan their items. They were purchasing six packs of beer, and as is the policy, I asked for their I.D. Back then, you had to find their birthdate and punch it in to the keyboard, and it would let you know if they were old enough or not to purchase alcohol. I matched up the picture I.D. with the person who was buying the alcohol and looked at the date of birth. Well, this time, I tried to mathematically figure it out on my own and "save time" by not having to punch it in. Wrong! Critical mistake. Not a good decision. The year was correct, but this person was still about two months away from their twenty-first birthday.

Mistakes are always going to be a part of our everyday lives, there is no way around that. But, this is one of those mistakes you never want to make, especially as an assistant store manager. I proceeded to finish scanning this customer's order and moved them along, completely unaware that I had made this critical error. As I was still checking out customers, two men walked up to my check stand from the front of the store, showed me their badges, and then proceeded to introduce themselves as Tobacco and Alcohol Enforcement agents, and they needed to talk to me ASAP. As you have probably figured out by now, I was in *huge* trouble. My heart sank, and the adrenaline flooded my system at an alarming rate. I was instantly in a cold sweat and wanted to hide from this reality of my failure to do my job.

You see, up to this point of my life, I was building my identity, my story. This management position that I had achieved is where I had chosen to put so much of my time, effort, money, sweat, and blood into. I started to believe that this promotion, this new position, would bring me the respect I thought I deserved and earned. I also believed it would make me look good, popular, well-educated, and successful. It gave me a sense of accomplishment, and it became my identity. Since I had no college degree, and I never went into the military out of high school—I really had no idea what I was going to do to make it in the world. I just winged it and hoped for the best. And, so far, this was my best.

I knew the few things that I had going for me was that I was an extremely hard worker, I was loyal, honest, and dedicated to becoming successful in whatever I chose to do or whatever path I chose to take. This was not part of the plan. I had plans of one day becoming a store manager with my own store. I was going to prove to everyone that I was not a failure. I was determined to succeed and win in this thing called life all on my own with nobody's help. Looking back now as I write this, I can still feel the insecurities of who I was and what I felt I needed to prove.

After the agents had approached me and told me they wanted to talk to me, I knew that whatever I had accomplished so far with QFC would be forever tarnished. I was losing my identity and instantly felt banished, alone, and a failure. I had just made one of the biggest mistakes you can make not only as a checker but even more so as a manager. As I was still in the check stand and still scanning groceries, I called the checker back from her break so she could relieve me. Since I had no idea the procedure that was about to take place after my fatal error, I proceeded to take the agents upstairs into the office so we could be somewhere private. This is where they began to explain to me what was going to happen next. Since this was a first-time infraction, there was no jail time, but there was a major fine to me and to the store.

As company policy was enforced, I had to call my store manager and inform him what had happened, and he immediately came down to the store and relieved me of my duties for the evening. I was suspended for a week with no pay, and the pain of absolute embarrassment was overwhelming me. Humility has a way of bringing things to reality. I was humbled, depressed, and started to think that maybe, this is not what I was supposed to be doing. I questioned everything after that, and asked myself, "Is this really what life is all about? Is this as good as it gets?"

As you can imagine, this one major mistake, set me on a course of disappointment and remorse. "What the heck do I do now?" Believe it or not, QFC continued to let me be a manager in the same position at the same store, but I was never able to shake the embarrassment that came from making that one fatal decision. That one mistake would most likely be branded on me for the rest of my managerial career with QFC.

Realizing this truth and the unwavering feeling I could not shake free from, I decided it was time to make a change. About two weeks later, I turned in my keys and stepped down from management. I had to walk away from this and my career. My drive, my confidence, and my ability to function as a manager were now in question, and I just couldn't handle the way that made me feel. About a year later, I quit QFC altogether and decided to start something new. Now, back to the beginning of my story . . .

In 2001, I began a new journey driving all over Western Washington in a big, long truck with huge Twinkies and Cupcakes displayed on the side of it. It was exactly what I needed, to get out of my head from my past mistakes and build a new career from scratch. After I began working for Hostess-Wonder bread, it took me about a year to get my own route. Up to then, I had been driving what they call "relief" routes. If someone was sick, on vacation, or jury duty, I took over their route as needed.

It was hard and laborious work. I know what you are thinking, "How can it be hard work tossing around Twinkies and Cupcakes with some Wonder bread thrown in?" Trust me, it was hard. When you pack into a rack a full assortment of snacks and then have about three to four racks to deliver, plus two to three racks of bread for just one stop, it adds up and becomes extremely heavy. Do that over and over again for about ten to twelve hours, and you will be exhausted— on top of the unfamiliarity of driving other people's route.

So, when the time came, I was very excited about finally having my own route that I could call mine and never have to do anyone else's for a change. My new route was in the heart of downtown Seattle. From up past Broadway to downtown on every street from Madison to the Puget Sound. It was a crazy route that would end up filling my days with unbelievable stories because of all I would see and hear. I saw so much homelessness, sadness, and loneliness everywhere, and it touched me to the core.

I usually got to the depot around 2:00 a.m., and after stocking my truck, I arrived at my first stop around 4:00 a.m. My first stop on this particular day was at a QFC on Broadway. If you are familiar with Broadway, it is a crazy part of town with the most interesting people. Lots of people that you could say are living on the "other side" of the tracks. These are the kinds of people that are looking to shock you with their uniqueness and differences of how they choose to live, look, and act. If you wanted to be different and fit in, this is where you would go. So with that in mind, I never expected to see what I saw one morning written on a sidewalk in chalk.

Now, I believe there are signs everywhere that could potentially be trying to get our attention and maybe even, by chance or by purpose, right there, just for us to see. I normally would pull up my truck to the right side of the road just across from the front of the store and park there. In these bread trucks, there is no driver's side door, there is just one main sliding door where the passenger would be, and this is where you are getting in and out of the truck.

It was dark, of course, and after I had grabbed my handheld computer, I opened the sliding door to step out and start my day. After opening the door and almost stepping out onto the sidewalk, I saw something that was written there, in chalk, directly in front of me right where my feet would land once I stepped down. It was even written in the direction I was looking. And it said this, "God has a plan for your life." Now, I know that this is not out of the ordinary. But to me, being in the area I was, and at four o'clock in the morning, it was a shock for me to see.

From the demographics of where I was, this would be the last thing I thought I would see written there on the sidewalk. But, there it was. I don't know about you, but these kinds of signs not only catch my attention, but really make me stop in my tracks.

After I opened that door to see these words, I literally paused and stood there reading them over and over again for some two minutes. I thought to myself, *What are the chances that I would stop exactly where I needed to stop so that when I opened the door these words would be right in front of me?* And with the words facing in my direction like someone had just written them there for me. I was extremely grateful for these words. I needed to hear them. I needed to know I was not alone and that God was really there, watching over me.

I believe we all want to feel and know that we have a purpose on this earth and in this life. To know we are not a mistake. That there is a reason why I am here, a reason why I was created. We are *all* in need of these truths and reassurances. Most of our lives, we are just trying to get by to survive. We fumble around this world trying to find our bearings so that we have some idea as to where we are going and what for. God, are you really out there? What do you want me to do? What is this all about?

Many of you who are reading these words are a lot like me. You have been there before or you are there right now, and maybe you have had this type of experience. Somewhere . . . out there . . . you have stopped for a minute to look up into the dark sky, filled with shiny diamonds, and wonder. In the Bible, it says that we are made in his image and that each of us are perfectly made. I do believe that, and I also believe that his love is so big that we just have a hard time fathoming that he is really that big, and that he truly loves us this much.

I have been blessed to have had the beautiful experience of hearing God's voice. As I have had the opportunity to share that experience with many other people, I have come to realize that this type of experience doesn't happen as often or to as many people as I would have thought. I don't truly have an answer as to why I was given the privilege to be called upon or even worthy enough by God to fulfill his purpose through me. Because, trust me, I have asked myself that question many times. "Why me God? What did I do or have I done to have been given such an honor as this?"

I believe we all have a purpose here on earth that God has created us for. A purpose designed especially for each of us and that matches up to our nature, our DNA, and our character to fulfill something only we have been created and chosen to fulfill. Throughout your life, has anything jumped out at you with more clarity and grabbed ahold of your heart like nothing else has? Have you ever felt drawn to something so strongly that it seems to mean more to you than anything else in your life?

I love collecting sports cards. It is one of many things throughout my life that I have found that I love to collect. Ever since I can remember, I have always loved collecting things. I have collected rocks, stamps, coins, posters, vintage Star Wars toys, records, autographed sports memorabilia, comic books, seashells, antiques, etc. My wife, of course, doesn't get it, but she still supports it. Which is why I love her so much. She is so supportive in everything that I am passionate about.

Besides having a passion for collecting things, I have always had a passion for God—a passion to understand and know him, and a passion to seek him and a passion to find him. I have chosen to put into my life a mission to grab ahold of him in any way that I can. This has not always been a successful mission as life has a way of getting in between God and myself. To choose such a mission is to choose to invest a lot of my life and time into reading books, prayer, Bible study, and being a part of church events. It has become, in a way, a collection, my passion and "My Milk." Something has to become so passionate to you, that everything else becomes a distant second place. I have experienced and seen how the things of this world, material things, can become our god if we allow them to be.

One of my gods at one time in my life was my vintage Star Wars collection. I dedicated a whole room in my house to this collection. For years, I collected this stuff. Scanning all the antique stores, toy stores, and flea markets hoping to find vintage toys from when I was a kid. My first find was a 1977 twelve–inch Darth Vader action figure that was totally complete with a red light saber and a flowing long black cape. It was really a doll, but we will call it an action figure. It was totally cool and after that find, I was hooked. It was a really fun time hunting for these rare items with my friends, finding them complete and fighting over them. Of course, this was before E-bay and Craigslist were created. It was the thrill of the hunt. But it cost a lot of time, money, and dedication.

After a couple years of collecting, and a lot of money spent, I had filled up quite a few boxes and plastic containers of stuff, and now, I finally had my room to showcase them in. I had all my autographed sports memorabilia intertwined within this room with movie posters all over the walls. It was killer. Needless to say, it was a sight to see, and all the neighborhood kids loved this room I created. I ended up putting in a big screen TV, a love seat, and a surround system in this room, and it was the bomb. It was the "Man Cave" I had always dreamed about.

Until, one day, I invited my pastor over to show him this room that I had created with all my cool collectibles in it. Although he was impressed, it didn't take long after he saw this room that he began to ask me some questions about it that instantly helped me to realize what I was doing. I was convicted of my sin because I had turned all my investments, time, and energy into this magical room of material things. This room had become my god! Not long after this truthful realization, the one true God put a different passion on my heart and he did something I never expected.

Sometime in the year 2004, I was sitting in church watching a video of my pastor, Monty Wright, and another gentleman, Bob Van Liew, who had just returned from Uganda in Africa. As a church, we joined together with World Vision to sponsor a village way out in the mountainous regions of Uganda in a village called Kasitu. They had brought back a video of their journey there and the kids they had met. By the end of that video, I was a blubbering mess. You know, because I am a crier and all.

Anyways, as I was sitting there in church crying uncontrollably, I heard God's voice say to me, "Don, I need you to go to Africa." Almost instantly, my body was covered in goose bumps from head to toe, and of course, I started crying even harder. In fact, I couldn't stop crying. I cried all the way home and I was still crying as I entered the house.

At church, after I heard God's voice, I answered him right then and told him, "I will go, Lord," and I just kept saying it over and over again. All I knew was, whatever it took, I had to get there. This is something that I will never forget as long as I live. To hear the voice of God is a moment in itself, a miracle. For a few seconds in this thing we call time, God reached in to my life and asked for something— something of significance and of great importance for him to decide to break into my existence and ask me to go somewhere for him.

Looking back on this event, it has brought me an incredible amount of Joy. It confirmed for me on many different levels that not only does God exist and is alive and well, but he is at work through-out many, many lives, and *is* answering prayers through us! With this example of God making himself known to us, shouldn't this increase our faith and our trust in him that his plans for us are perfect and beautiful? If we could just get out of our own way for a moment, Jesus then would have a chance to reach in and change our lives in some of the most radical ways that we couldn't possibly imagine. I was about to find out how truly radical that was going to be.

Now, around this same time, I had started sponsoring a child through World Vision and his name was Godfrey. He was around six or seven at the time when I started sponsoring him and his family through World Vision. What a joy it was to receive letters and pictures of him in the mail. I would write back to him and send pictures, too. I learned a lot about him and his family and their village.

About a year later, my pastor informed the church that they were planning a Mission Trip to Uganda in 2006. As soon as I heard that, I was the first to sign up. But now, I had to figure out how I was going to raise $4,500 over the next year.

We had our first Africa Mission Trip meeting, and they gave us some ideas on fundraising, basically telling us to start sending out letters to everyone we knew asking for cash donations to help with the cost. Unfortunately, this didn't make much of a dent in the amount I needed to raise. So, I began to improvise and brainstorm on how I was going to fill in this massive gap of money that I still needed.

One day, as I was standing in my garage evaluating all my belongings, an idea came to me. All these things were just sitting in my garage never being used and collecting dust. How much money could I make if I sold all this stuff sitting in my garage? That is when I decided I was going to have a yard sale. Then I thought, *I wonder how many other people have stuff they really don't want sitting in their garage*. That is when the first yard sale was born that started it all (more to follow). The idea was a huge motivational jolt for me, and I was off and running. I typed up a one-page letter to my neighbors explaining what I had planned to do with this fundraising yard sale and what it was all about. In the letter, I explained how much money I needed to raise, and that I needed their help. I explained to them that I needed their donations, so I could put together a big enough yard sale to raise enough money for me to go and hopefully help others to go also.

Finally, I went out with about 250 letters and handed them out, door-to-door, to all to my neighbors where I lived at the time and their stuff started pouring in. As I was collecting donations in my garage, another vision came to me. What about all this stuff you have in your Star Wars room? Why don't you sell some of that stuff? Sure enough, as I was standing in the room looking at all this "stuff" I had collected and spent thousands of dollars on, the hard truth began to surface. The Holy Spirit was having a tug of war with my willingness to let go of my material treasures. I had to come to the harsh reality of my collection and what I had to do next. Although it started small as I began to dismantle the things I cared least about, over time, I was then able to slowly release the things that mattered most.

I had spent a long time and worked so hard to attain these rare and vintage toys. I would say to myself, "I earned them, they're mine, and I don't have to let them go!" Sound familiar? I instantly think of Bilbo Baggins from *the Lord of the Rings* and the "ring of power" he hung onto for so long so many years. He never went anywhere without it. And when it was time to let it go, he couldn't, and he fought to keep it. Gollum, who owned the ring before Bilbo, also struggled to let it go. In fact, Gollum was so obsessed with the ring that his obsession to get it back drove Gollum to his death. It became a god to Bilbo Baggins and also to Gollum.

These rare collectibles, the expensive Star Wars vintage toys that I once held so close to my heart, began to lose the value that I once believed they had. My heart was being transformed. I soon learned that over four thousand children under the age of five were dying each day in Africa due to the lack of clean water and sanitation. I began to see the eyes of the children in Africa and the suffering they had to endure. I would envision looking out my front window of my house, and there lying in my yard were four thousand dead bodies of African children who had died because of contaminated water. This inspired my determination, and my heart began to break for the things that breaks the heart of God. As more and more heartbreaking information came to my attention, the more I saw these collectibles and rare toys as money to get me to Africa and hopefully more than that. Maybe I could possibly change a life or maybe even save a child!

As the yard sale grew and grew and donations filled up the Star Wars room and my two-car garage, we then began to fill up a moving truck. As the yard sale date approached, everything was full and now being piled up in front of my garage under a huge tarp. In late July of 2006, in my driveway, my yard, and on my sidewalk, the Snoqualmie Valley Alliance Uganda Mission team came together and built this huge yard sale that, in three days, raised over $4,300. It was such an amazing event, and God moments were happening everywhere.

One of the most amazing things that happened were the cash donations being given, and sometimes people didn't even buy anything. They just wanted to give. One lady, who I didn't even know, came up to me and told me she wanted to make a cash donation. Now, I was under the impression it would be $50 or maybe even a $75 cash donation. Nope, not even close. She handed me a check for $1,000. I instantly lost it. My heart leaped, and my soul filled with intense love. I started sobbing, and I grabbed that woman and hugged her ever so tight. She told me that "This was for the children," and through my tears I kept saying to her, "Do you even know what you have just done, do you know what you have done?" I was blown away, sobbing uncontrollably. And then she turned and walked away. Quite a few of us from the mission team cried that day from the generosity of so many people's hearts. I still get emotional thinking about that moment when I knew that God had stepped in. His fingerprints were all over that yard sale that weekend, and I knew then my life would never be the same.

I learned something very special that weekend, too. When you move in the direction of God and his calling upon your heart, your life will be filled with extreme moments of the deepest love and life-changing events that you will never forget. You will be transformed, changed, and life itself will be magnified. You begin to see the world with different lenses. My purpose and my passion began to evolve and to become clarified as God moved again and again on this incredible journey of love.

What is your *milk*?

This was only the beginning of an adventure that is still going and is as strong as ever. I truly believe that each and every one of us is created and destined for great and amazing things. The key to the Great Adventure, as Steven Curtis Chapman would call it, is to turn your eyes to the prize. The more you become aware of what is truly important in this life, the more your eyes and heart are opened to the truth. The prize is Jesus. When you make him your number one priority, then and only then does the adventure start.

> The day you take a step of faith and hand the control of your life over to God is the day you take your first step to peace, freedom and pure joy.

The selfishness of a human heart is very bloated, stubborn, and full of wickedness, greed, and sin. Mine included. We as humans, and especially men, struggle to understand what it means to "let go and let God." We want to control our own lives. "We don't need anyone to help us with this thing called life. I got this. I am completely in control." What a crock of balderdash that is. I had always been out of control, but for some reason, I never wanted to give up control. I would give Jesus my life and then take it back again. I am not sure if it is out of fear, stubbornness, or just my lack of faith in him. No matter what we hear, and what is preached to us, we simply cannot or will not let go of control of our lives. But that is where it has to start. The day you choose to take a step of faith and hand the control of your life over to God, is the day you take your first step to finding what it means to have peace, freedom, and pure joy.

Please hear me and understand, this is going to be one of the hardest choices you will ever make. Each day at the start of your day, you will have to remember to purposefully hand over your life to Jesus. *This is not about religion.* I cannot make that any clearer than this. Our faith in Jesus is based on a relationship with him. You cannot earn your salvation. It is a free gift. When Jesus died for you and for me, he basically stretched out his arms and showed us how much he truly loves us and wants us to be in a *relationship* with him.

His grace is enough for every one of us, every day. No one is out of reach of Jesus. No matter how much you believe you have done in your life, you will never be exempt from his love or forgiveness. He came and died for the lost, the hurting, the weak, the despised and the broken, all of us. He came and died for those who are struggling with addictions, whose lives are so full of remorse, shame, guilt, sadness, and loneliness. He came for the Ragamuffins of this world as Brennan Manning so lovingly puts it. We are *all* Ragamuffins who need Jesus in our lives.

"It is not the healthy who need a doctor, but the sick. I have not come to call the righteous, but sinners to repentance" (Jesus, Luke 5:31–32).

No matter how rough around the edges you think you are, Jesus doesn't care and loves you just as much as the saints. I know that I am a ragamuffin who was once weak and has now been made strong. Temptations will always be a part of life and the struggle we will fight against every single day. The beautiful truth is, is that Jesus loves you, will always be here for you, and wants you. He knows what you are going through and has even experienced some of what you have been through while here on earth.

He was despised, rejected by his fellow men, hated, abandoned, arrested, and left alone to be mocked, ridiculed, beaten, tortured, and eventually killed—all because he loved us and wanted us to know our heavenly Father. His death on the cross became the bridge that would forever open up the possibility to love and have a relationship with him. This is the good news, and this is why billions follow him, love him, and even die for him. We have the one true hope in our eternal life with him . . . all because he chose to suffer and die for our transgressions, our poor choices, our pain, our struggles, our addictions, and our sin.

One of my favorite things to do is to listen to or read of the stories of the testimonies of the lives that Jesus has touched, changed, healed, and transformed. Some of the stories I have read and listened to would curl your toes, make you cringe, and bring tears to your eyes. Don't ever believe the lies of the evil one who only wants to keep you down and out. Jesus loves you more than you will ever know, more than I will ever know! But here is the greatest news of all. Jesus has already done all the work!

You don't have to do anything. All you have to do is make a choice to step in the direction of the greatest love on earth and in heaven. Believe in the name of Jesus as God's only Son and cry out to him. Tell him that you're sorry for all that you have done and that you want him to be in your life. Ask for forgiveness and be cleansed of your sin by the blood of Jesus. I guarantee you will never regret this choice, and you will never be the same. God does not want to force his will or force his love on us. He gave us freewill to choose for ourselves what we want in this life. I don't fear death or destruction. I know where my soul is going. The question is, do you?

When I drove for Hostess-Wonder bread in downtown Seattle, I learned firsthand what it meant for these brothers and sisters of mine who were hungry and thirsty, who needed clothes, and were sick. The homeless everywhere are people with their own stories of struggle and pain, loss, and loneliness. When Jesus walked the earth, these are the people he hung out with most. He loved on them like no one ever before or after, healing everyone along the way, loving, and cherishing everyone no matter their walk of life. I have tried to emulate Jesus in this way, and it is humbling. I have not always succeeded, but I have always tried to see them as people who have just fell on hard times. Every one of them has a story to tell, and they are just as valuable and worthy as anyone of us.

I had the privilege of befriending a homeless man in Seattle while working down there for two years. He would get so excited when he would see me coming down the road, and I always had spoils on my truck of Hostess brand snacks that I gave away every chance I could. Not exactly the healthiest of food groups, but at least they wouldn't go away hungry. This friend of mine was such a neat guy, and I really enjoyed talking with him. It is a whole new world down there and what they have to put up with. He would usually be in need of some very basic things, so I would bring him shoes and socks whenever I could, and he was always so grateful.

One day, with tears streaming down his face, he gave me this huge hug and just kept telling me, "Thank you, thank you." I will never forget that hug as long as I live because in that instance, in that moment, I truly felt what it must have felt like to be Jesus. Not that I was Jesus, of course. But this man, filthy as all get out, felt comfortable enough to open his arms and show his appreciation and love for my simple gifts. I will tell you that at first, I was a little nervous about hugging this man who was this dirty. But once we embraced, I felt the love of this man, and I didn't care about any of that. All I cared about is that he knew I loved him and cared for him. This is what it means to love with the love of Christ.

"Jesus was coming down a mountainside and suddenly a man with leprosy approached him and knelt before Jesus. 'Lord,' the man said, 'If you are willing, you can heal me and make me clean.' Jesus reached out and TOUCHED HIM. 'I am willing,' he said, 'Be healed!' And instantly the leprosy disappeared" (Matt. 8:2).

Wow . . . just wow!

This story is one of hundreds that moves me and touches my heart. The fact that Jesus reaches out and touches this man with leprosy is an amazing story. Lepers were considered the lowest of lows in Jesus' time and leper colonies kept them at great distances and outside of the city grounds. The lepers had to yell "Unclean!" everywhere they went so as to give all the other people a head's up when traveling about so they could get as far away from them as possible. I know this is nowhere close to my experience of hugging this homeless man, but this is what I had thought of when I did.

How many times do we move away from people like this? How often do we ignore them and pretend like we don't see them? When we begin to understand the love of Jesus in our lives and in our world, we begin to see a much brighter and more beautiful picture of what loving each other truly means. I felt this love between two men of different walks of life but equal just the same in the eyes of Christ. And now in my own eyes as well.

I am telling you this story not for my glory, but because I only want to give God all the glory. And I am telling you this story so you will have an example of hearing about the love of Christ in our crazy world of selfishness and loneliness.

"Whatever you have done for the least of these brothers and sisters of mine . . . you did for me" (Jesus).

My views on life, politics, social media, and everything in between has become less important to me because of my belief and understanding of what really matters in this world. You can easily get wrapped up in all that is going on in the world, or you can see past it all to the deepest, most important parts of what this thing called life is really all about.

How many of you that are reading these words understand how fast time goes by? So, if you understand then, how fast time goes, wouldn't you want to do all that you can with the time you have been given to make an impact in this world? Let them who have ears to hear, let them hear. Life is too short. Sometimes, it is over way before it should be. None of us has any time to spare, and none of us knows how long we truly have on this earth. I don't want to waste time and energy on things that don't matter to me, things that will truly never change or will never make a difference.

So, I guess, it comes down to what is the most important thing or passion to you. What is your *milk*? My only suggestion is to take a long hard look at what that passion, or mission, or God is. Are you making an impact on this world in a negative or positive way? Will what you have done on this earth be felt by people after your time here on earth is done and you have passed away? Have you made a difference in the world or in the lives of people all around you?

The Pharisees tried to trick Jesus by asking him the question:

"Teacher, which is the most important commandment in the Law of Moses?" Jesus replied,

"You must love the Lord your God with all your heart, all your soul, and all your mind. This is the first and greatest commandment. A second is equally important: 'Love your neighbor as yourself.'" (Matt. 22:37–39)

This and many more verses in the New Testament are wrapped up simply by saying that we are to love each other. This is exactly what Jesus taught us, showed us and commanded us to do. The more I read his Word, the more I see and understand the simple beauty in what he said. Love truly conquers all things.

"Dear friends, let us continue to love one another, for love comes from God. Anyone who loves is a child of God and knows God. But anyone who does not love does not know God, for God is love.

God showed how much he loved us by sending his one and only Son into the world so that we might have eternal life through him. This is real love—not that we loved God, but that he loved us and sent his Son as a sacrifice to take away our sins. Dear friends, since God loved us that much, we surely ought to love each other. No one has ever seen God. *But if we love each other, God lives in us, and his love is brought to full expression in us.*

And God has given us this Spirit as proof that we live in him and he in us. Furthermore, we have seen with our own eyes and now testify that the Father sent his Son to be the Savior of the world. *All who confess that Jesus is the Son of God have God living in them, and they live in God.* We know how much God loves us, and we have put our trust in his love. God is love, and all who live in love live in God, and God lives in them. *And as we live in God our love grows more perfect. So we will not be afraid on the day of judgement, but we can face him with confidence because we live like Jesus here in this world. Such love has no fear, because perfect love expels all fear.* If we are afraid, it is for fear of punishment, and this shows we have not fully experienced his perfect love. *We love each other because he loved us first."* (1 John 4: 7–19, emphasis added)

Throughout God's Word that he spoke to us and through his Son, Jesus Christ, we can experience the greatest of gifts and that is unconditional love. Nothing on earth is more powerful and life-changing than love. I can express with all the truthfulness I can muster, that nothing on earth has brought me more joy, more love, more forgiveness, and no greater feeling in the world than the love of Christ showering over me when I least deserved it. And because of that unwavering love, I will serve him always until the end of my days.

I was a severely sad and broken man with years of pain piled on my shoulders. I carried that and all my other failures, poor choices, and sin along with me, my burdens, for a long time. I had believed the lie that I was unworthy of his love until one day he showed me the truth. And throughout my life, he has had to remind me over and over again of this important truth. Jesus told me I was worth it. He told me I was worthy of his love. And when I finally listened and believed, when I finally understood what he did for me, I fell to my knees in glorious joy, sobbing uncontrollably with a shower of love and forgiveness I cannot explain. From my head to my toes, I felt a cleansing of spiritual proportions that could only be from God.

I think it is important to have direction. To have goals and purpose. To what extent are you willing to find that purpose in this thing called life? I have read a lot of books that have had an incredible impact on me, my choices, and my life. I love books and the truth we can find in them. The list of books I am about to share are books that are very close to my heart and within their pages I have found intense truth, love, and beauty. I found these books to be incredibly enlightening, and they are books I highly recommend reading—especially if you are searching for truth, for understanding, and for wisdom. I have read some of these books many times, and I have learned so very much from them. Please consider finding these books and dive into the love that is within them because they are truly life changing.

- The Shack by William P. Young
- The Case for Christ by Lee Strobel
- The Case for Faith by Lee Strobel
- The Case for a Creator by Lee Strobel
- Primal: A Quest for the Lost Soul of Christianity by Mark Batterson
- The Hole in Our Gospel by Richard Stearns
- The Ragamuffin Gospel by Brennan Manning
- The Jesus I Never Knew by Philip Yancey
- What's So Amazing About Grace by Philip Yancey
- Same Kind of Different as Me by Ron Hall & Denver Moore
- When the Game is Over It All goes Back in the Box by John Ortberg
- And of course, the Bible by God

These books have helped me to see not only how much God loves me, but how much I need to love those that God loves, too. I have spent a majority of my studies of the Bible primarily in the New Testament. For me, this is what I needed most throughout my life. I have found that the words and truth of the New Testament resonated with me to such a deep level and it was a guide, a light onto my path. The New Testament scriptures is one way that God can speak to us and he uses them to show us the way through life and all of its challenges. For someone who is searching for answers about God or you are a brand-new Christian, I would suggest starting here, in the New

Testament. Then as you grow in your faith, branch out to the Old Testament, as well.

It is never too late to make a change, to revamp your life, to seek out and find how you can make a difference either with your natural gifts or talents or by just finding something that can bring light into this dark world. There are endless ways to spend your time and money—spend them wisely! Choose to love those who are left out, who are forgotten. Choose to find ways where you can invest your money into someone's life and feel the joy in how that makes you feel knowing you might have just changed a life for the better. Sponsor a child, or two, somewhere in the world either through World Vision or some other organization. Give hope to the hopeless, and love to the loveless. Be Christ in this world. Hug more often, say nice things, give to those in need, lift people up, and let them know they are beautiful and wanted and worthy. There is *no* greater feeling in the world when you see the tears of someone whose life you have just changed for the better. Even something as little as holding the door open for them can go a long way. Branch out, take risks, and live life to the fullest.

People need to be loved. It is one of the most basic needs of our human existence. People need to feel that they are wanted and appreciated. People need to know that they are important and not forgotten. People. We are *all* people—all the different nationalities, different colors, different accents, and different walks of life. Love each other. We may have different lives, different beliefs, different backgrounds, and different stories, but that is what makes us unique. Love everyone. Always remember, you have no idea what someone may be carrying around their whole life and how heavy that baggage might be. You have no idea what their story is and how much pain they have had to endure.

A compassionate heart will always go so much further to find ways to love the unlovable. The world does not revolve around you. This life and the things that are in it are just things. Stop focusing on things and start focusing on people and how you can make their life better. We are here to love each other and love God. Period. You have a purpose and a passion. Now, go find it, and live it with all you've got! You will never be the same when you choose to love those who need it. Turn your calendar, turn your pocketbook and your heart in the direction of those who are hurting and dying. Show them love by your *actions*, not just by your words.

> Walk as children of light and try to discern what is pleasing to the Lord. Take no part in the unfruitful works of darkness, but instead expose them. For it is shameful even to speak of the things that they do in secret. But when anything is exposed by the light, it becomes visible, for anything that becomes visible is light. Therefore it says, 'Awake, O sleeper, and arise from the dead, and Christ will shine on you'. Look carefully then how you walk, not as unwise but as wise, making the best use of the time, because the days are evil. Therefore do not be foolish, but understand what the will of the Lord is. (Eph. 5:8–17).

CHAPTER 4

I Named Her Trinity

Never doubt that a small group of thoughtful committed people can change the world. Indeed, it is the only thing that ever has.
—Margaret Mead

Christianity has always insisted that the cross we bear precedes the crown we wear. To be a Christian one must take up his cross, with all its difficulties and agonizing and tension-packed content, and carry it until that very cross leaves its mark upon us and redeems us to that more excellent way which comes only through suffering.
—Martin Luther King Jr.

The movie, *Schindler's List*, directed by Steven Spielberg, is a movie based on the true story of Oskar Schindler during the holocaust and the sufferings of the Jewish people in probably one of the most horrific and horrible times in our history. There are hundreds of stories of incredible people doing heroic acts of love and kindness through such a tumultuous time during World War II. This is one of those stories.

Businessman, Oskar Schindler, played by Liam Neeson, arrives in Krakow, Poland in 1939, ready to make his fortune from World War II, which has just started. After joining the Nazi Party primarily for political expediency, he staffs his factory with Jewish workers for similarly pragmatic reasons. When the SS begins exterminating

Jews in the Krakow ghetto, Schindler arranges to have his workers protected to keep his factory in operation, but soon realizes that in so doing, he is also saving innocent lives. This truly amazing man is credited with saving the lives of more than 1,200 Jews during the Holocaust by employing them in his enamelware and ammunition factories, which were located in occupied Poland.

This true story reflects his life as an opportunist initially motivated by profit, who came to show extraordinary initiative, tenacity, and dedication to saving the lives of his Jewish employees. After exhausting all his resources, he sells all he has and bribes the SS officers to keep the factory running.

When the war finally ends and the Jews are set free, Schindler is now the one being hunted for being part of the Nazi Party. The Jews he saved are now working hard to make sure he gets out of Poland without being arrested. As Schindler is getting ready to leave, he begins to say goodbye to all his factory workers, all the Jews he saved from the death camps.

This is when it finally dawns on him what he has done and to the extent of how he saved all these lives. He crumbles under the weight of how incredibly important life truly is, even to the expanse of losing everything he owned. Schindler soon realizes that he still has a car that he could have sold and saved ten more lives. He begins to cry as he finds a lapel pin that symbolizes his membership in the Nazi party attached to his jacket that is made of gold and realizes he could have sold that gold pin and saved two more Jewish lives. As he is sobbing and crushed by the actions and love he gave to save every Jewish life, he continues to sob, saying, "I could've saved two more lives . . . I could have saved two more." This scene and really the whole movie is an amazing portrayal of how much it means to value human life and how others don't value it at all. I, of course, was crying watching this Oscar-winning movie, and I absolutely loved it. The list of all 1,200 Jews working in the factory became a symbol of life, survival, and love.

Two years after I heard God's call to go to Africa, my opportunity finally arrived in October of 2006. And after a successful yard sale in my own front yard, I had raised enough money to pay for this trip and help others in our group who were lacking the funds to make it to Africa. After many months of planning, praying, organizing, and prepping, we were finally ready to go.

One of the main concepts I had prepared myself for was to have no expectations on this mission trip. I had no selfish desires other than to meet my sponsored child, Godfrey and his family. I prayed that this mission trip would continue to transform me, mold me, and help me to grow and understand humility. I don't believe there would have been anything I could have done to help me prepare for what was coming. Unsurprisingly, I was extremely excited and anxious to see why God had personally called me on this mission. I opened my heart and my mind to try and be free from anything that could block what I was to hear, see, and feel. I knew this would be a trip of a lifetime and I was about to be blown away.

"Whatever you did for the least of these . . . you did for me" (Jesus).

I had been on many flights before this trip to Africa. I had been to Hawaii, Mexico, other states, and even Great Britain for a different mission trip. But this trip was going to be twenty-three hours of flying in a twenty-nine-hour trip with a six-hour layover in Amsterdam.

By the time we landed in Entebbe International Airport, Uganda, my feet felt like balloons. They became bloated and extremely uncomfortable, but I knew there would be sacrifices and physical ailments involved on this journey. Before this, I had to get a total of seven shots in both arms so that I could even be in Africa!

We landed in the early evening, and off to the right of the airport was a gated animal reserve with giraffes walking on by with their long necks swaying back and forth with every step they took. Although we had chosen to come at a time when it was the rainy season, this evening was dry and humid. Since all our transportation needs had already been prepared through World Vision, we only needed to get through customs and then be on our way. I remember it being somewhat of a culture shock when I was walking through the airport and the different checkpoints, getting our visas stamped, and going through security. It really felt like being in a movie, or at least what you see in the movies when they are in a third world country.

Once we had our luggage, the thirteen of us climbed into Land Rovers and vans to take us to our next destination, Kampala, the capital of Uganda. Bordering Uganda was the second largest lake in the world, Lake Victoria. One of the cool facts we learned about Lake Victoria was that out of Lake Victoria flowed the beginnings of the Nile River. The Nile River is a north flowing river that flows from Lake Victoria all the way up to Egypt and into the Mediterranean Sea.

I will never forget the scene on our way to the hotel after we left the airport and the sun went down. As we drove through town after town, we noticed that hardly anyone had electricity. In fact, no one had electricity. We saw nothing but candle after candle lighting up the windows of houses as we drove along. It was a humbling sight to see. This is the beginnings of what it means to live and grow up in a third world country. We arrived to our hotel, which was surrounded by a huge gate and armed guards. We were unsure as to why there needed to be guards with rifles, but needless to say, we felt protected.

It was late, and it was straight to bed after we got to our rooms. The next morning, I was the first one up, and I was very excited to see what I couldn't see the night before. As I exited out the back of the hotel onto the terrace near the swimming pool and lounging areas, the sun was just cresting over the horizon and it was breath taking. Huge streaks of red and orange completely changed the whole skyline into these brilliant shades of color. I walked out a bit to get a better look at everything and almost instantly was startled by these humongous birds flying directly over my head. There were about twelve of them with their wings outstretched and legs sticking out straight back away from their bodies. Gloriously beautiful and it was a tremendous sight to see. They came in for a landing right in front of me, about twenty yards away.

As I later found out, these large birds were the Marabou Storks, and they were everywhere. They seemed as abundant as pigeons in Seattle. They were all over Kampala, and they made huge nests in trees everywhere we went. They stand over five feet tall and have a wingspan of more than ten feet. No wonder I was a bit startled when they flew over my head that morning!

After I breathed in all the beauty of the incredible views of nature I had the privilege of seeing, I settled down to have some Bible time and prayer time. Today was a day of recovery from such a long flight, and boy did I need it. We all enjoyed the down time and got caught back up on our sleep and adjusted to the time change. It messes with your body when you fly that far for that long, and I struggled the whole flight to even sleep at all.

I love taking pictures . . . I always have. I got my first real film camera, a Canon, in eighth grade, and I have never stopped taking pictures since. I took several film and camera classes in middle school and high school, but now I had a digital camera and could take a ton more pictures. I snapped pics almost continuously while in Africa. If I wasn't taking pictures, I was taking video of our trip. That was one of my main goals while being there. I wanted to capture as much as I could to bring back home to share with everyone what we saw and experienced. Uganda, no doubt, delivered some beautiful scenery and animal life. I came home with some gorgeous photography.

Later that day, we went on a tour of Kampala, and we saw amazing and wonderful things. The children, of course, were the highlight. Everywhere we went, they were waving and smiling at us. To see the children so interested in seeing us and so full of joy was beautiful and enlightening.

The poverty was just as I imagined. The red mud and clay anthills were enormous, and some were taller than me. We eventually ended up at the World Vision Head Quarters in Kampala. While there, we had to participate in a few seminars covering everything from HIV-AIDS to dress code, sponsorship, and visiting with our sponsored families.

We hopped back into our World Vision transports and began the six-hour journey to our final destination, which would be the village of Kasitu. Before we took off for Kasitu, we were told that we could no longer wear shorts of any kind, and the women had to wear dresses that came down to their ankles. Men had to wear slacks, jeans, or cardigan pants. This became challenging as the humidity did not ever subside. There was always a glow that came from everyone's faces because of the constant sweat. But we dug in and knew beforehand this was going to be the designated attire for most of this mission trip. It was a small price to pay for the privilege of doing God's work.

From Kampala to Fort Portal, which was the last civilized town we would see, there were paved roads, and it took us a couple of hours to get there. After we arrived in Fort Portal, we stocked up on any food or water we needed before taking on the hardest part of the trip. In the small grocery store were many recognizable items we see every day back in the states, but didn't expect to see here. We saw Kellogg's Corn Flakes, Lay's potato chips, and they even had

Red Bull. I bought a bag of rice and a doll to add to the gifts I had brought for Godfrey, his siblings, and his mom and dad.

We took in the surroundings of this last civilized town as we knew that where we were headed next would have nothing close to this. But even in this town, the bathrooms consisted of a single small room with a door and a hole in the dirt ground.

It started raining just before we left that town, and it seemed like it never stopped till we came back around six days later. Not only did we leave civilization, but we also left paved roads. It was nothing but dirt and rocky roads from here venturing up and over the mountainous regions of Uganda—a four-hour trek through dense jungle, mountains, and deep valleys.

I will never forget the noises of the jungle—thick with the sounds of a substantial amount of insects and animals. The monkeys we saw and the vines hanging from the trees were so cool. just like in Tarzan. The views were incredible as farmers had their crops on the sides of steep valleys, and we had to go around huge long horn cattle being driven by cattle hands on these treacherous rocky roads.

Many times, we would be looking down the cliffs on our right side as we would pass people walking. We also had to pass very large trucks overloaded with passengers when there was only room for one vehicle. It was crazy and seemed rather dangerous at times but that only added to the exhilaration of this adventure.

When you step out in faith with action and advance in a direction that seems crazy . . . that is when you know you are truly living. I believe this is exactly what and where God wants to take us. He wants us to take chances and step into the unknown, to trust him, and move in a direction that will challenge us and stir up our souls. Up to this point, I had never felt more alive than when I took this challenge to come here. The Great Adventure, by Steven Curtis Chapman, kept running through my head throughout this trip. I knew this would truly be the beginning of life I had never quite experienced before. This was a huge stepping-stone into a brave new world. I also knew that my heart was going to be broken like it had never been broken before.

One of the things I remember reading in one of my favorite books was a line that someone used that has never left me and keeps me asking this question over and over. "Does your heart break for the things that breaks the heart of God?" It is a question we all should be asking ourselves. Are you compassionately embracing the pain of the broken hearted and the people that are hurting like God is asking us to? Or are you purposefully ignoring the cries of the helpless, the hopeless, and the homeless?

Let me back track a bit here and go back to the hotel in Kampala. The second day I was there, I was again sitting outside in the lounging area of the hotel, listening to Don Henley's greatest hits watching the people walk by and wondering what was in their heart. I was feeling their pain, or at least, I could see their pain and their burdens on their faces and in their body language. I wanted to reach out and grab their hands so that maybe, they could get a glimpse of the love of Jesus flowing through me.

At another table nearby was a young African woman who was shy and looked to be about seven–eight months pregnant. It was obvious that she was upset, overwhelmed, and carrying a heavy burden. I felt the nudge of the Holy Spirit to go sit with her and talk with her.

I found out her name was Faridah and she lived in a town called Kibuli. As I conversed with her, I found out that sadly, her boyfriend had kicked her out of his home because she became pregnant, and he wanted nothing to do with her. This young woman's parents were also disgusted with her and did not want her in their home, either. She was in a very dark place, and I comforted her as much as I could.

I asked her if I could pray for her, and she said yes. After I prayed for her, she asked me who this Jesus was. She said she had heard of him, but really didn't know who he was. This opened the door for me as I sat and talked with her for a good hour or two. It wasn't easy because she had quite the accent and didn't speak English very well.

I asked her if she had ever read the Bible before, and she said no. So I gave her my Bible, and she began to read it out loud. It was so elegant and beautiful to hear this young woman with a beautiful African accent, read God's word for the very first time. She wasn't quite ready to accept Jesus into her heart, but the message got through, the seed had been planted, and she got to read and hear about him. I read to her verses from the New Testament that talked about his love for us and his sacrifice on the cross. She was very grateful for our time together, but before she went on her way, I wanted her to know that she was loved. I had the privilege of giving her a Bible and some money. We hugged and cried together then said goodbye.

I will never know how this divine interaction turned out, how it affected her life, and if she ever gave her life to Christ, but hopefully I will when we get to heaven, and we will see each other again.

These are the kinds of risks worth taking. If we don't ever step out of our comfort zone and into faith, then we may never see the kingdom of God, here on earth. Unless we are ready to put on the armor of God and get ready to fight the good fight, then the battle has already been lost. I don't know about you, but I want to win the prize, and I want to run the race and finish strong until the end when either Jesus calls me home or when he returns in his Glory.

Take chances, take eternal risks, and grow in your faith. I would highly suggest you take them and believe in him and yourself. This life is only a blip in time, and I want so much more than this ordinary life. No one is going to give it to you, you must take it by the horns and steer it in the direction of your desire and passion. But pray that the passion that is inside of you will be for the kingdom of God one way or another.

> Everything is pure to those whose hearts are pure. But nothing is pure to those who are corrupt and unbelieving, because their minds and consciences are corrupted. Such people claim they know God, but they deny him by the way they live. They are detestable and disobedient, worthless for doing anything good. (Titus 1:15–16)

Thousands and thousands of lives, millions, need us now. They need *you* now. My hope and my prayer is that through me, through my example, through my actions, and my story, somehow, God will use me to reach just one person for Christ, if not many more. I would love to give hope to one person or save just one child with the Love of Jesus. By his wounds, we are healed!

I was passionately living my life for Christ when he called me to do this mission and obey his calling to go to Africa. And now, here I was, in the middle of nowhere, in the jungles of Uganda, hours away from civilization. I was being blessed with the privilege of entering into a most primal situation, which in turn would change my life forever. This, my friends, is *living*.

As we reached the peaks of the mountains we needed to pass through, we then began a downward trek into the valley on the other side. We could see for miles and miles the jungle valley before us and eventually our destination. As we got closer and closer to Kasitu, the more enthusiastic we became. We truly had no idea what to expect or what we would see, and we wondered if there would be people there to meet us or just the World Vision employees to greet us.

Our hearts grew more and more anxious to see why God had brought us this far and what he was about to show us. Years of waiting and wondering were about to explode in front of our eyes and in our hearts, and we were struggling to hold back the excitement.

God did not disappoint us as we entered into the village of Kasitu. In fact, He blew us away once again. Six hours later, after we had left Kampala, we finally arrived, and we were greeted and welcomed like nothing I could have ever imagined. With hundreds of kids everywhere waving and singing, I instantly felt so much love that I was flooded with tears. I didn't even make it out of our vehicle and kids were already smiling and waving at us. What a glorious welcome it was. When I finally did get out, the singing was just so beautiful with hundreds of kids all singing "Welcome to Kasitu" jumping with elation. They also had signs that the kids made for each of us. Mine said, "Feel at home Don." The tears just flowed uncontrollably and didn't stop for a while. I actually did feel at home like I was supposed to be there. I was overwhelmed, but I felt and thought nothing else but the love that I had for these children, and it was glorious! I was completely lost in their lives and in their world, and I could have sat and talked with them for hours and hours. The love and eagerness in their eyes was unbelievable. As I read in my journal from that very day, twelve years ago, this is what I wrote:

> I have first-hand seen the effects of giving and it is more beautiful than I could have ever imagined. It truly is better to give than to receive. I only want to give more. What else can I do to change these children's lives? What else can I sacrifice? What else can I let go of? What else? I know I can do more, and it is up to me! Take that step of faith—step in the direction of Christ and store up more treasures in heaven. I know God is smiling down on me. I know he is happy. I only want to continue to shine for my Lord and Savior. I love you, Jesus!

So six years later, I would get the call to fulfill the words I wrote in my journal previously. That, I will explain later in another chapter.

We arrived at the World Vision Area Development Program headquarters, the A.D.P., with a rundown building that the W.V. employees were able to use. It is nothing fancy but gets the job done. This is where they conduct their business, plan, organize, and distribute letters to the children who have been sponsored through W.V., and it is also housing for those who have been hired on by W.V. To see what this organization does for these children and their families was extraordinary. I have a huge amount of respect for how far they go to meet the needs of these impoverished people and especially the kids.

In their beautiful accents, they would sing over and over, "Welcome to Kasitu . . .welcome!" Once they were done singing, we got to greet them, talk to them, and shake their hands, which just made them even more excited. They loved seeing their faces in our cameras and video recorders, and they would just laugh and giggle.

The poverty, as I had expected, was pretty bad, and some children's bellies were protruding out because of malnutrition, but still they seemed as joyful as ever. Most children were without shoes or proper clothing. There were also a lot of children carrying babies on their backs or in their arms.

What was also so beautiful and unbelievable at the same time were the people. I saw Jesus in their eyes. I saw hope and thanksgiving. I felt their love and delight, and we just gave it right back to them. As the children were dancing and singing, one of the older children came up to me and asked me to dance and sing. She said, "You dance, you sing." So I sang to them and danced for them, and they just shrieked with pure joy. They thought that was the funniest and coolest thing they ever saw!

While there in Kasitu, I wanted every child and every person to know that we loved them and cared about them. I wanted them to know that they will not be forgotten. We saw many skits performed by every age group, acting out life and the challenges that they face every day such as HIV and AIDS, the misconduct of unwanted sex, and the challenges of poverty, hygiene, and clean water.

After all was said and done, we then headed to the next town called Bundibugyo (pronounced Bundy-boo-ju) where Hotel Vanilla was. Hotel Vanilla was where we were staying while visiting Kasitu and its surrounding villages. This was the only place that had any power of any kind and that power was from a generator. We each had our own room with a shower and toilet. No hole in the ground, surprisingly. The shower ran with cold water, and we didn't have any lights until 6:00 a.m., but this was better than I had imagined it would be. Over our beds were mosquito nets so the mosquitos wouldn't bite us at night. I was grateful for that net as I slept because the mosquitos were everywhere buzzing in my ears all night. Malaria was still a major cause of death in children in Africa, and W.V. was able to distribute malaria medicine to kids who were currently sponsored. Recently, one of Godfrey's siblings had become very sick and had to have medicine administered to them otherwise they might have died.

At 8:00 a.m., it was already getting warm, and I was dressed in my Khaki pants and a nice button-down shirt. Today's events revolved around going to church and then visiting two different schools. One near Kasitu and one that was up in the hills. The first school was run-down but had all the necessities to make it work. They had benches and big long tables to do their schoolwork on. Big chalkboards in the front of the class with English letters, numbers, and words everywhere. They also wrote words all over the walls of the classroom. The kids were so delighted to see us and just kept saying, "Hello, how are you?" They loved getting a response out of us, and it really seemed to make them happy. They were hanging out of the wooden windows of the school laughing and screaming. So much fun!

The next school we visited was way up in the hills just below the mountain peaks. We would have never made it there if it wasn't for the Land Rovers. Sometimes, we would just drive off the road into the bush that was actually taller than the trucks we were driving in and make our own roads to get where we were going—crazy and fun.

When we did finally arrive at the other school, again, we were blown away. After we had parked our vehicles and started our way up the dirt road to the school, the children had lined up on both sides of the road in their bright yellow dresses, yellow and baby blue shirts with their teachers welcoming us, singing to us, and playing their drums. Again, it was a sight to see, and it only brought more tears to my eyes to receive such a gracious welcome. The kids had different colored shirts and dresses depending on which grade they were in. They were gorgeous colors ranging from yellow to baby blue to forest green. W.V. provided these beautiful school uniforms, and they also rebuilt the school up there on the hill. We saw firsthand the change and the difference that we had begun to make in the lives of the people of this region of Africa. They were so grateful, thankful, and full of love for us. It was truly incredible.

Once we finally got to the school, they had chairs lined up for us outside. Off to the side was a table with soda pop waiting for us. They were really making us feel like royalty. There on this beautiful hillside with the sun shining, with God's glorious creation all around us and the mountains standing with thick, beautiful vegetation everywhere, the whole school began to sing to us songs that melted our hearts and brought us to tears once more. The kids in their colorful uniforms lined up around us with this breathtaking view of the Ugandan valley jungle behind them. With their arms raised high and in their graceful and inviting African accents, they began to sing to us this song while drums played in the background:

> I love you, Jesus.
> Sit down into my heart.
> I love you, Jesus.
> Sit down into my heart.
> Deep to deep
> Down to down

Sit down into my heart.
Deep to deep
Down to down
Sit down into my heart.
I love you, Jesus, sit down into my heart.
I love you, Jesus, sit down into my heart."

My heart was so full of love and appreciation that I was beginning to think that I was going to cry tears of love and joy nonstop on this trip. After they were done singing for us, I was so in awe, full of so much gratitude for all they had done for us. I yelled and screamed with joy with whoops, and the kids laughed and loved that very much. After that particular time, the kids would copy me with that same whoop and excited noise and just laugh and laugh. Then we presented for them duffle bags of school supplies, soccer balls, and jump ropes, which they were all very electrified about. Once we were done, we said our goodbyes and headed back down the dirt road to finally meet our sponsored children and their families.

This, of course, is what we had all been waiting for and were filled with great excitement and anxiousness to meet our children. Most of us, if not all of us, had sponsored children here in Kasitu, and when you sponsor a child, you are really sponsoring the whole family. The child gets to go to school and is provided a school uniform, medicine if needed, food, and supplies.

We came to a stop just off the dirt road and parked. We knew we had a bit of a hike through the jungle terrain up the mountain trail to reach the first house as the rain drops started to fall. It was about a one-and-a-half-mile trek up that trail, and it wasn't long before we started to get pounded with large drops of rain at the onset of a storm. And it was a mighty downpour!

According to African culture, if it rains, that means your visit will be blessed. Well, we were truly blessed—we were beyond blessed. We were all given the greatest gift from God on this journey to see our sponsored children. We were all getting drenched as we made our way up the trail. On both sides of us just a few feet off of the trail were many forms of jungle vegetation with the sounds of insects and jungle noises. Some of the folks were grabbing huge leaves off the indigenous trees and using them as umbrellas. To me, it was like something straight out of a *King Kong* movie.

We stopped half way up and used some cover from a house nearby, but realized we had no choice but to keep going until we made it to our destination. The trail up the mountain became very muddy and very slippery. A good portion of the time, we had to hang onto each other so we would not slip and fall. Most of us were already covered in red clay and mud up to our calves, but we were loving it all the same. The sound of the giant raindrops in the jungle was just beautiful, and the smells were intoxicating. It took all I had to not start belting out the song from the group Toto, "I bless the rains down in Africa!"

On the way up this trail, I was busy taking photographs, video-taping, and just trying to stay with the group the best that I could. I was at the very end of the group because I was stopping to take so many pictures. In doing so, I failed to notice that there was some-thing on my left, just a few feet away from me, crawling out of the jungle, just off the trail. When I finally turned to see what was mov-ing, I was startled to see that it was a man who was walking on his hands dragging his body behind him. Because I was focused on the pictures I was taking, I didn't see him or hear him until he was right up next to me! As you can imagine, I was shocked, and I couldn't believe what I was seeing. This poor man was paralyzed from the waist down and had no other choice but to drag his body behind him everywhere he went. He was drenched, his hair was long and stringy, and his face covered in dirt. His eyes looked hollow and without hope. He wore sandals on his hands instead of on his feet where they served his purpose.

I was instantly saddened and had deep compassion for this man; yet, I could do nothing for him. He put his hand out as he balanced himself with his other hand and said nothing. Regretfully, I had nothing I could give him. I had no money, no food, nothing, not even a Bible. I felt horrible about this, but I had to keep moving. However, it was a sight I will never forget.

It gave me a glimpse into what Jesus must have seen a lot of in his day—people with all sorts of ailments and sickness crawling up to Jesus crying and begging for healing, for love, for hope. I later wondered why this woefully crippled man came to me. Why was I the one who had to see him? And why did I not stop, lean down, put my hand on him, and pray for him? I regret that I did not pray for him.

Finally, we made it to the first sponsored family, and they greeted us with such gratitude, humility, and thankfulness. Shaking all of our hands with both of theirs. Sometimes giving hugs and smiles all around. All of us went inside their mud and stick home and watched as Christine visited with her sponsored child and her family. It was life-changing. Tears were flowing everywhere as we took in this beautiful exchange of love between people from two totally different parts of the world. All in the name of Jesus. They were just so thankful for what we were doing for them.

As it was with every sponsored child, we gave them the gifts we brought for them, and they would in turn give us something they had for us. The gifts I saw ranged from things they had made by hand to Adirondack chairs, to mats, to even a live chicken. Each moment with each family was extremely special, unique, and lovely. As we made our way back down the mountain, it dumped on us again and we were completely soaked from head to toe with red mud up to our knees now but still basking in the glory of the adventure. And what an adventure this was turning out to be! I believe I cried, as did everyone else, at every house we went to.

Next up was Susan Edward's family, and this time, we separated from the other group so we could all go meet our sponsored children. Susan Edwards, Susan Graham, and I jumped into the Toyota with Elvis (who was the ADP leader of the group), Johnny, our driver, and two W.V. translators, Hope and Robert. As we arrived at the home, the grandmother greeted us with so much love and thankfulness. On the interior walls of this mud house were drawings made from chalk of people, trees, a helicopter, and words in English. Susan's sponsored child, Shalon, came into the room wearing a pink dress with a huge smile on her face. The two of them were so excited to see each other. There were hugs shared, introductions, and greetings abound.

There were no parents to be found, just the very grateful grandmother and her six grandchildren. We were so moved and touched by their love and generosity, and yet, they had so little and still wanted to give so much. They gave Susan a chair, and Susan gave her sponsored girl a necklace and a bracelet among many other gifts that she absolutely loved. The exchange put a huge smile on her face from ear to ear.

As we sat and visited with them, we soon learned from the grandmother that she was the sole provider for her six grandchildren. The grandmother has had the most unfortunate situation of having to bury all nine of her children, which was just overwhelming to even fathom. The loss and sadness in her life is just so hard to even understand. To have been given the responsibility at her age to raise these six grandchildren after nine of her own children died is simply hard to swallow. This is how it is though, this is the reality in families all over Africa. HIV/AIDS is wiping out entire generations of families, leaving over ten million orphans in its wake. Susan prayed with her sponsored family, and then we had to say goodbye with tears in our eyes.

We then ventured on to visit Susan Graham's sponsored girl and of course it was just as emotional and surprising. As it was before, we climbed into their small mud and stick home and crowded into a small room with just the door opened providing light into our little gathering. Susan saw her sponsored girl, Patrice, right away, and there were hugs, love, and excitement everywhere. Not long after that, the mom came in wearing a beautiful yellow dress with a bright purple headdress, and she was so grateful that she couldn't hold her excitement and thankfulness for Susan's love and sponsorship. She gave Susan a big hug and then another with great joy in her voice.

We later had another visitor walk in to surprise our group. Patrice had a twin sister that Susan knew nothing about! Her sister joined Susan on her other side and more hugs were given. Eventually, Susan was able to sponsor her twin sister as well, which gave Susan even more joy in her heart. As we sat and visited with this mother, we eventually found out that she also had another set of twins—two younger boys and one older daughter. Sadly, we found out later that her husband had been diagnosed with HIV/AIDS and was going to die soon. The mother, we also learned, eventually contracted the disease from her husband.

A year later, along with her husband, the mother of these five children also died from HIV/AIDS. This mother, so full of life and joy, was taken too soon. The orphans were cared for by World Vision and Susan's sponsorship. Their aunt took over raising them. World Vision built them a brick house that we were able to see under construction on our second mission trip to Uganda a year later.

With great joy and enthusiasm, it was finally my turn to visit Godfrey and his family after such a long time waiting and wondering. We drove through dense jungle, long grass, and through some deep mud, and finally arrived at the entrance of a trail that followed along the edge of high grass and trees. As the African rain continued to pour, we headed down the trail that led to Godfrey's house. The trail was so thick with mud, our feet kept sticking as we made each step. When we finally turned the corner, I could see through the jungle brush some mud and stick houses and people rustling around. It was a small group of houses, about eight or nine, in a clearing of the jungle.

Before we arrived at Godfrey's house, I became anxious, but inside, I was calm and at ease. As I neared the entrance, I instantly found Godfrey, and he saw me and we both smiled ear to ear. He came running to me, and we gave each other this huge hug like we had known each other for a long time but hadn't seen each other in a while. His hug felt instantly like I had just found a child of mine that I had never knew. He grabbed ahold of my hand and held it tight as he walked me over to meet his mother. She was so giddy and so excited to see me that she literally could not stand still. She was very beautiful with this amazing smile, and she glowed from the humidity. When I finally made it over to her, I gave her a huge hug and a kiss on the cheek, which made her squeal with animation. It was quite humorous.

What surprised me though was that she was carrying a brand-new baby, not more than a couple months old. I then shook hands with his dad who was very polite and grateful, and finally his siblings who also were very excited that we were there. All the neighbors came to share in the event and greeted us as well.

As we all piled into their small house and proceeded to do more introductions, the rain started pouring again with only the soft light of the open door shining on Godfrey and myself. We sat around a small wooden table with Godfrey on my left, in the shadows was his father next to him, and then his mother with the baby girl and his siblings sitting between them. The translators were sitting by the door, and Susan was standing next to the open door videotaping because there just wasn't enough chairs or room to sit.

The anticipation and excitement of this journey to meet them had finally come, and it was a challenge for me to hold back the joy that was in my heart. I had brought two backpacks full of gifts for Godfrey and his family, and I was very anxious to finally give them what I had brought all this way just for them. I pulled out two soccer balls, one for Godfrey and one for his siblings, baseball caps for his dad, which he loved so much that he immediately put one on his head. I also brought binoculars for Godfrey who had a difficult time figuring out how to even use them. Once he did, he looked through them out the door, and he had this huge smile on his face because he had just experienced something he never had before. I also brought Star Wars action figures, a photo album, a mirror, and so much more. I became very aware, very quickly, how different our lives truly were.

The items that I had brought with me, these people have never seen before. Most of these people living in Africa have never even seen their reflection except maybe in a mud puddle. To look at a photo album full of my kids' pictures was a treasure to them. When I had given Godfrey's mom the jewelry and the scarf I brought for her, she squealed again and smiled ear to ear clapping her hands as she held her baby girl.

The family gave me some rice they had planted and three chicken eggs in a plastic bag. That is all they had to give, and I was very grateful. I remember thinking that I couldn't possibly take this food from them. They needed it more than I. But the translators told me that it would be an insult if I did not take it, so I did. They of course were all very grateful for the gifts, but what happened next would forever change the course of my life.

As you already know, I had been writing letters to Godfrey and his family for close to two years now before I finally got to fly half way around the world to see them. But what I didn't know was that when I arrived to see Godfrey and his family, his mom had recently given birth to a little girl. This beautiful baby couldn't have been more than two months old. So after I had given them their gifts, Godfrey's parents began to talk with Hope, the translator, telling her something in their native language. As I waited patiently to get the translation, I noticed, by the look on their faces, that Hope and Robert were a bit surprised by what Godfrey's parents were actually saying to them. When Hope finally turned to look at me, I was now quite curious as to what it was they had said. She began to tell me "How happy they were that I am here and how grateful they are for all I am doing for them." Then she said, "They have been excited and waiting for you to get here because they want you to name their baby girl!"

Wait, what?

As you can guess, I was completely blown away once again. I was in complete shock and did not know what to say or what to do. Susan Edwards completely lost it, and she began to cry. I was instantly covered in goose bumps as my heart and soul became filled with intense love. I cried with such joy in my heart, but I also knew I had to try and pull it together and not completely lose it. I knew I didn't have much time left with my sponsored family, and now, I had to come up with a name for this baby girl, and I only had a few minutes left to do so.

After much pressure and a limited amount of time, I could only think of one name for this baby so, I named her Trinity, after my own daughter. I couldn't believe what an incredible honor it was that they had given me. This was truly a God moment, a gracious gift from God. I was completely overwhelmed with gratitude, thanksgiving, and love for this family. And again, it only showed us how much of an impact we were making in this family and every family that sponsorship touches.

Before my time was done with my new family, I was able to hold baby Trinity in my arms and kiss her and love her like she was my very own. Then to seal the deal, she pooped through her cloth blanket, because they have no diapers, straight into my hand, which I thought was only appropriate!

With tears in my eyes and my heart flooded with love, I was able to pray with and for my family and it was absolutely beautiful. I felt I was given another family by God, and they welcomed me as their own. As I left my new family I hugged them all, and I gave Godfrey's mom another kiss on the cheek, and she squealed some more with excitement. I told them I loved them all, and I hope to see them again soon. I will never forget them and the gift they had given me.

What was crazy to realize and understand is we thought we were coming to Uganda to give to them, but it was just the opposite, they gave to us. These people had given us so much more. We knew that making this trek to Africa was a huge deal to them, and we saw how much they loved it and appreciated it. We just had no idea how much it would end up impacting us.

When we had returned from our trip to see all of our sponsored children, I told everyone what had happened. We all embraced, crying with love and joy in our hearts for all that God was showing us and giving us. Everyone had amazing stories to tell, and we all felt like we had just been given the greatest gift of all in having the opportunity to see and meet our new adopted families.

I literally was a mess from that day on and for months to follow. I tried to tell this story of baby Trinity without crying and just couldn't do it. And usually, the person hearing the story ended up crying with me. It truly was the most incredible God moment that happened to me on this trip, and it left a mark of love that would forever transform me. I can honestly say, I have never been the same since. This "Journey of a Thousand Tears" simply opened my eyes to see so clearly all that God wanted me to see, and I grew exponentially on that mission trip. My heart, my soul, and my faith grew even more. There was so much that I had seen and experienced that my heart broke so many times for the things that breaks the heart of God.

The next day, I wrote Godfrey and his family a letter about my feelings and thoughts of our beautiful time together—to let them know how much they mean to me and how grateful I was for the gift they had given me. I also asked Elvis for a Ugandan Bible, which he was able to find and delivered it to them along with the letter.

As we were packing up the transport vehicles to head back to Kampala, four different people came up to me and asked me for a Bible. And, again, I asked God, why me? Three of them were employees of the Hotel Vanilla. There was Betty, Locus (who read John 3:16 for me in his amazing accent which was awesome), another server whose name I didn't get, and then Ahmid, who was the driver of the W.V. transport van and who was also Muslim, which I thought was simply incredible. I only had two Bibles to spare, and so I had to hunt down two more. What a delight and honor it was to meet that need and how sad it is to think that they don't have the accessibility or the finances to even purchase a Bible.

The evening before we left for Kampala, we had one last meeting at Kasitu World Vision headquarters with Elvis and the A.D.P. staff. First, Elvis was amazing—what a heart for God and a deep love for the people. The staff was simply a Godsend. Their commitment, hard work, organization, and love for these people—simply unmatched. We all fell hard for these World Vision workers for God. Johnny, our other driver, was the best, and I love that brother. Hope and Robert were just so patient, informative, and they were just awesome. "God is good, all the time" is what they would say over and over throughout this trip. No doubt, God is so very good.

The next day we headed back to Fort Portal and almost everyone in the van was giving me a hard time about naming Godfrey's baby sister. As I processed all that I had seen and experienced, it continued to amaze me, the special gift I had been given. I was so humbled and so very grateful by this act of love. I was very ecstatic to share this story with my family and to everyone who would stop and listen.

As I finally made it back to the other side of the world, it was extremely difficult for me to get back to my normal way of life. I was forever transformed from what I had seen and was exposed to. I had a hard time trying to function, trying to work, and not feel completely helpless to what I saw. The question that I had to ask myself over and over again was, "What was I going to do about it?" Everything I saw now, everything I did, I had to look at through God-peeled eyes. God had peeled from my eyes all the western civilization way of living and thinking and showed me the depths of pain, suffering, and loss that was taking place in just one small part of the world.

Life was hanging on by a thread in Kasitu, but there was hope in their eyes and God in their hearts. We had the privilege of meeting an eighty-year-old grandmother who lost all nine of her children and was raising her six grandchildren all by herself. We witnessed a ten-year-old who was raising his two younger siblings because they lost both parents to HIV/AIDS. We found a very sad little girl sitting in her front yard who looked like someone had stolen her soul because she had lost both her parents to HIV/AIDS. We met a mom with five young children whose husband had just died of AIDS and was worried sick that she has also been exposed to this deadly virus. A year later, it took her life as well leaving her five children orphans. I literally saw a man crawl out of the jungle, dragging his body behind him all the while walking and pulling himself by his hands.

Through one of the heavy, torrential rain storms, I was filming the lightning and thunder with all the rain pouring down and flooding the streets with rivers of water. As I pulled around to the side of the ADP building, I found a woman standing below a waterfall of water shooting off the roof of the building. She had with her two, huge, yellow five-gallon jugs sitting there, and she was filling them up from the fountain of water spilling off the roof. This being the cleanest water she could find for her family, she took full advantage of that opportunity. Once she was done filling them, she lifted one in each hand, and proceeded to make her way through the alley of two mud houses and was ankle deep in streams until into the distance, I saw her no more.

As I was filming this woman standing there, soaking wet, walking in this torrential storm, with sixty pound jugs full of water in each hand, I sat there in absolute amazement and awe as to the extent of what these people have to go through every day of their lives to survive. This water that this woman was collecting was the freshest and cleanest water she could get for her family. Most families, and it is usually the moms and the kids, have to walk up to six miles to bring home a couple gallons of diseased and contaminated water each day. Seeing this woman do what she was doing broke my heart. I knew that going home from here was going to be difficult. My life would never be the same again.

After all this, it took me years to get back into the swing of things, and it only took God five years to come calling again. You see, God had called me to go to Africa because he had an even bigger plan for my life. Bigger than I could ever imagine. In fact, even as I write this book, I see that this was also a part of his plan, of course. I never thought I would ever write a book, not in a million years.

All of my experiences in this thing called life have transformed me over and over again. I can guess with a pretty good accuracy that this adventure will never end until he is done with me, and then I will have served my purpose here. "God has a plan for your life"— that message I found, written in chalk years earlier, kept coming back to me. In my obedience, I was fulfilling his plan for me, but that was only the beginning, there was so much more he wanted from me.

Looking back on these memories and experiences really took me back to an amazing time in my life. To remember some of these moments I had experienced and the names of the people I had met, I had to break open my journal from my mission trip to Africa from 2006. One of the prayers I had written down said this:

> I am overwhelmed. I pray, Lord, that you can help me through this process. It is a lot for me to swallow and I only want to give you Glory, Lord. Use this story in every way possible. Give me the wisdom, Lord, to translate this amazing journey of love and giving into hope for more African children and their families. Crack open the creativeness to maximize the possibilities of what I can do for these people. My love and my willingness to improve their lives goes very deep. I know this has been a time for growing for me, Lord, and it hurts. May I never lose focus. Give me strength to overcome the world and all its temptations. This is our purpose, this is our mission—our mission for Christ. To preach to all the nations the powerful name of Jesus Christ. To bring hope to the hopeless, love to those who are without love and fulfill all of God's great pleasure. November 8, 2006

"If you want a sense of mission to burn brightly in you, spend some time feeding your divine discontent. Usually we try to avoid unpleasantness, but if you have a sense that your mission involves helping the poor, spend time around those in poverty, allow your emotions to become deeply engaged and carry with you that fire that things must change!" (John Ortberg, When the Game is Over It All Goes Back in the Box)

Light that fire and let it burn brightly. If you feel a calling on your heart, and that passion is burning inside you to make a difference, go after it with a sense of urgency and with a tenacity that nothing will stop you. You will never regret it and your life will never be the same!

The four gospels, Matthew, Mark, Luke and John, repeat one saying of Jesus more than any other, "Whoever wants to save his life will lose it, but whoever loses his life for my sake will find it."

This saying has been proven to ring true to me over and over again. When we choose to let go of our life, our ambitions, and our selfish desires, then and only then do we start to really experience life in its fullest. Life is suddenly more peaceful, beautiful, and free. My soul is flooded with love and purpose, and all the problems of our chaotic lives becomes less. Step in the direction of love, giving, and purpose, you will never feel more alive than when you move in the direction of losing your life for the sake of Jesus, so you can save it.

"We make a living by what we get, we make a life by what we give" (Winston Churchill).

CHAPTER 5

BUILD IT, AND THEY WILL COME

Dear Children, let's not merely say that we love each
other; let us show the truth by our actions.

—1 John 3:18

Set out each day believing in your dreams. Know without
a doubt that you were MADE for amazing things.

—Josh Hinds

Once we realize that Jesus has served us even to the
depths of our meagerness, our selfishness, and our sin,
nothing we encounter from others will be able to exhaust
our determination to serve others for His sake.

—Oswald Chambers

On August 14, 2012, I was reading a book titled *Primal* by Mark
Batterson. That book and its contents sent me on a whirlwind of
emotions that to this day, is continuing to unravel God's glorious
calling on my life. Through that book, my heart and soul were being
dismantled and broken down, once again to hear the cries of children
who needed help, who needed love, and who needed hope. That day,
on August 14, I heard God's voice again calling out to me ever so
abruptly, and my heart was breaking again for the things that break

God's heart. This time, God was calling me to do something incredibly radical and primal.

He revealed to me a vision and a plan to put together the biggest yard sale anyone has ever seen and from that yard sale, we would raise enough money to build a lot of clean water wells that would save children's lives. I wrote in that book on that day in 2012, "I pledge to you, Lord, to put on the largest yard sale ever and donate all proceeds to missions. We shall take nothing and give everything! For eternal hearts and lives. Save the children! I pledge to raise $15,000 for your children." That was the day that started me on the next *Great Adventure,* and it hasn't stopped since.

"Every act of generosity creates a righteous ripple effect that can change the course of history. It will also change your heart" (Mark Batterson, Primal).

When God gave me that vision and I could see it in my head, I was instantly electrified with excitement, and I knew this would be something very special. It had been five years since I had last been to Africa. In 2007, a year after my first mission trip to Africa, I went back again, and this time, I was given the honor of leading the group. It was another amazing trip filled with so many God moments and memories, but I was still a mess from all that I had seen and experienced before. And like I had said before, it took me a long while to recover from that first trip.

I was now in the middle of a divorce and was shaken to my core from where my life had now come, since my last mission trip to Uganda. I was struggling to find peace again and purpose. Drastic failures like divorce are a heavy blow to your overall view of what you wanted and hoped for. I never imagined that this is where I would be once I had chosen to get married and have children. I believed that I was making a solid choice, that I was emotionally and spiritually ready, but this is life, and I was not even close to being ready.

In the process of mourning the loss of my marriage of eleven years and the pain my kids would have to endure, I had to dig deep and continue to believe in myself. I constantly had to remind myself that I still was a good dad to my children and that I was still worthy of love and respect. That eventually, I would get through it all and know that God still loved me and still held me in his arms. Life is never easy, and the pain of life will come and challenge you at every turn.

The day that I heard his voice once again, I was brought to my knees in tears. I also knew full well that because he was calling me, I better be listening and getting ready to be obedient to the call. I had no idea how I was going to initially pull this off, but I trusted God, and I was pumped up for this challenge. I got to work right away to pull together all the information I needed or had already accumulated in my life. I then began to start planning, organizing, and processing all I would need to pull off this Giant Yard Sale.

> That is why we never give up. Though our bodies are dying, our spirits are being renewed every day. For our present troubles are small and won't last very long. Yet they produce for us a glory that vastly outweighs them and will last forever! So we don't look at the troubles we can see now; rather, we fix our gaze on things that cannot be seen. For the things we see now will soon be gone, but the things we cannot see will last forever. (2 Cor. 4:16–18)

There is no one exempt from pain, trials, and tribulations. It is a part of life. You either grow from that experience, or you continue to suffer in the pain and title of a failure. I have done both of these scenarios many times in my life, and I can tell you from experience, just let it go—get up, brush yourself off, and start the painful but rewarding process of forgiveness. Forgive yourself, forgive those who hurt you and ask for forgiveness of those you have hurt. Do not seek revenge, do not seek to cause more pain or anguish to someone else or to yourself. Dig deep and grow. Seek to find resolve and reconciliation.

These are the qualities of maturity and growth. If it wasn't for God showing me the way, I would be in deep doodoo right now. I love how God lights the pathway out of our darkness with his love and truth. Here I was, second-guessing my value and worthiness in the eyes of God, and He chose to call me out, humble me once again, and set me on a course of pure love and purpose to bring glory to God. It is pretty clear that God always knows what is best for us, even in the worst times of our lives.

After I finally grasped ahold of the belief that I was ready for this endeavor, I moved forward to make sure this yard sale was going to be a success. I began to share my vision with people at work and almost everyone I would run into. And at the beginning of January 2013, I posted to Facebook my intentions of building this giant fundraiser, and then the fun began.

I gave this much thought over the winter months, and I figured I was going to need at least six months of time and a ton of donations to pull this off. I created an event page on Facebook and invited all my friends and family to this event. As I did years before, I wrote up a page describing all that I was planning and hoping to do. I made hundreds of copies and carried them around with me while I worked at North Bend QFC and handed them out to all the customers and coworkers I came across over the next few months. I also knew that I would need an immense amount of storage to handle the amount of donations that would be coming my way.

So, I began the tedious task of driving from one storage unit company to another throughout the Snoqualmie Valley asking for free storage unit rentals. The generosity of the valley started pouring in, and I was able to secure five storage units free of charge all the way up to the day of the yard sale. Then the phone calls and text messages started to flood my phone, and the donations started coming.

I was spending almost all my time after work, before work, and on my days off, collecting donations or meeting people at the storage units to drop off donations. I began filling up storage units rather rapidly and with really good stuff. I was getting Facebook messages almost daily with folks who wanted to donate their stuff to this cause and the word was getting out. I eventually had to get creative to find new ways to raise money to help pay for rental trucks, gas money, and for advertisements. A friend of mine suggested the idea of change jars, and I instantly went to work to put these together. I bought a twelve-pack of quart size, ball-canning jars, slapped a sticker of a picture of me in Africa with a bunch of kids around me and a small story of what I was doing, then stuck them in businesses around the Valley.

People were generous enough to donate to those jars, which in turn helped pay for a lot of the gas that was being accumulated from all the donations I was picking up. I was borrowing trucks from friends like Fritz Ribary or renting U-hauls every week, and I soon filled up one storage unit, then another, and then another. I knew that I was running out of room and needed to get ahead of the game and started asking friends and family if they would be interested in sponsoring a storage unit.

I had some friends offer up their garages and my church, Snoqualmie Valley Alliance, helped me get another storage unit, and this went on for six months. Miracle after miracle, people I didn't even know wanted to help by sponsoring a storage unit.

Eventually, one way or another, over the next six months from January to July of 2013, I had filled up eleven storage units full of donations, and I had secured a site to have this enormous yard sale. I found a huge piece of open blacktop at North Bend Elementary, which was gated on almost every side. I also was able to secure the parking lot, which solved all my problems for making this work. I was finally getting close to the end of this crazy but amazing adventure, and I was tired and exhausted.

The local paper and the Issaquah paper somehow found out about it and wanted to run a story on the Save the Children Yard Sale. This was great for publicity to help us make this as successful as possible. I had hung up posters and fliers all over the valley and also put an ad in the Seattle Times and Valley Record listing this sale. I was determined to raise that $15,000 if my life depended on it.

My next move was to find and recruit enough people to not only help me put it together but also to help me run this ginormous sale. I had eleven storage units of donations that had to be loaded into moving trucks and then off-loaded into the elementary playground. I had reserved four moving trucks and also accumulated and borrowed 60+ folding tables to place all over the black top of the school. This was a huge undertaking, and I needed to make sure that every area was covered.

The moving began toward the end of July 2013, almost a year later after I heard God's voice. We started early on Wednesday morning to empty every storage unit and we didn't finish emptying them until Friday morning of the second day of the sale. We were blessed with so many great friends who volunteered and came to help in every area. We had cashiers, truck drivers, loaders and unloaders, people who folded clothes, supplied tables everywhere, and helped organize the yard sale as stuff came off the trucks. I was so thankful and so blessed to have my mom, my brother, Dave, and my son, Dalton, all by my side each and every day, helping me accomplish this amazing fundraiser, so we can save the lives of children who just need clean water to drink. We had people working in and around the yard sale answering questions and helping customers and replenishing and organizing tables as product sold. Every night, a bunch of us would camp out there and play games and sleep under the stars.

It was all an incredible sight once all the donations were put out onto the tables and around by the fences. For five long days, we hustled and grinded in the hot sun to make this all come together pouring bottles of water over our heads almost every hour because of the heat. We even had bands come in and sing and had a hot dog stand selling hot dog lunch specials, which were donated from Costco. I also invited World Vision to come and set up a table, so we could hopefully get some children sponsored.

All in all, it was an incredible success, and we had pulled it off. God had given us five straight days of hot and beautiful weather. In fact, the day after the yard sale was over, and we had everything cleaned up, it rained, which didn't surprise me one bit.

A community of love had come together to make a difference in the lives of thousands of children around the world and even in our own community. When it was all said and done, we had accomplished getting six children sponsored through World Vision, and we had raised over $25,000 dollars in the Save the Children Yard Sale—$10,000 dollars over my initial goal. As the days of the yard sale were flying by and the money was being calculated, I never stopped to think much about how much we were raising. I was too busy running the Yard Sale that I didn't really stop to think about it. But I will never forget when someone walked up to me to report that we had just hit the $20,000 mark. In shock of that reality, I began to break down and just cried like a baby, hugging onto my best friend, Todd Van Cise. It was a moment I will never forget—to hit a milestone like that absolutely blew me away. With God's help, I knew then we had all done something extremely special.

God showed up in that yard sale time and time again. We had so many people who showed up and made cash donations of $500, $250, and every other monetary amount you can think of. Miracle after miracle, this was proof to me that when you turn your eyes and your heart toward God and his kingdom, he will bless you abundantly.

"Be imitators of God, therefore, as dearly loved children and live a life of love, just as Christ loved us and gave Himself up for us" (Eph. 5:1–2).

I was seriously a mess for days after it was all done, and it took me three weeks to recover from it all. I believe God was smiling down on us. I took this calling on my heart with great joy and with a tenacity that would not be broken. Many days, throughout that time of collecting donations, I had to call on many people for help. And many people answered that call for which I will be forever grateful. Many times, I would be sitting at the end of an empty truck in front of a storage unit amazed at what was taking place, all the while thanking and praising Jesus for such an honor as this. This became my mission to change lives, save lives, and give them hope for a better life.

"You must each decide in your heart how much to give. And don't give reluctantly or in response to pressure. "For God loves a person who gives cheerfully. And God will generously provide all you need. Then you will always have everything you need and plenty left over to share with others" (2 Cor. 9:7–8).

Many other miracles happened at this yard sale. I had an abundance of clothes and books collected and an organization called Clothes for the Cause bagged it all up and took it away. They grabbed all the shoes, duffle bags, bedding, clothes, and books and even paid me over $500 for it all. We had another gentleman drive up with a huge truck and collect all that was left that had metal in it, which was over half of what was left. That was a true miracle because I had about ten TVs left just sitting there, and he took them all along with everything that was made of metal. Lastly, I had an army of volunteers that believed in this yard sale and gave their time, efforts, and hearts to this calling, to this mission of love and of giving. They believed in the vision God had given me and followed it through to the end. With their sacrifice, their love, and their commitment, we all went the distance to make a difference in the lives of children half way around the world. Their light shined ever so bright, and their love was present and beautiful.

I will always remember their sacrifice and love for such a wonderful cause. After the initial $15,000 was distributed to a wonderful and local organization, Planet Changer, which is the organization through whom all the clean water wells were built and constructed in Uganda, we used the other $10,000 for other local organizations to help meet some of the needs in our own community.

It was a huge weight off my shoulders when we finally finished this incredible calling. I also knew that this would not be the last time I would be doing this, and that my purpose still had just begun. Looking back on it all, it makes sense that God would have called me to do this because of my past experience with yard sales. It is amazing to realize how God had orchestrated all of this from the beginning. His calling for me to go to Africa in 2003, my yard sale in 2006 that raised $4,300, my yard sale in 2007 that raised $3,500 for my second mission trip to Africa, and finally this calling to put together another one that would top them all. He believed in me and helped me believe in myself. He gave me direction and a purpose that propelled me to step outside myself and reach further than I had ever reached before. And he broke my heart so that I would understand why he was calling me, and so I could also know what it feels like when it breaks the heart of God.

People have often asked, "How did you keep going and stay motivated to finish this till the end?" I would tell them that since I have been to Africa, and now know personally how they are suffering, knowing that over four thousand children are dying each day because of the lack of clean water—*this* was my motivation, and I needed to do this and finish this so that my life would not be in vain. This, all this, was *not* about me, but all about Jesus. My life was full of purpose, love, and joy because I knew that this was giving glory to God. You see, once you understand the big and beautiful wide-open picture, you start to see heaven here on earth. God's love is all around us and is being distributed through thousands upon thousands of people who love God passionately to the people throughout the world who are crying out to God for help. This, my friends, is pure love. This is the love of God being poured out through his servants, through his church, and through people like you and me. Every act of love will set you free.

> What good is it, dear brothers and sisters, if you say you have faith but don't show it by your actions? Can that kind of faith save anyone? Suppose you see a brother or sister who has no food or clothing, and you say, "Good-bye and have a good day; stay warm and eat well"—but then you don't give that person any food or clothing. What good does that do? So you see, faith by itself isn't enough. Unless it produces good deeds, it is dead and useless. Now someone may argue, "Some people have faith; others have good deeds." But I say, "How can you show me your faith if you don't have good deeds? I will show you my faith by my good deeds." (James 2:14–18)

CHAPTER 6

BY HIS WOUNDS, WE ARE HEALED.

One of the criminals hanging beside him scoffed at Jesus, "So
you're the Messiah are you? Prove it by saving yourself—and
us, too, while you're at it!" But the other criminal protested,
"Don't you fear God even when you have been sentenced to
die? We deserve to die for our crimes, but this man hasn't
done anything wrong." Then he said, "Jesus, remember me
when you come into your Kingdom." And Jesus replied,
"I assure you, today you will be with me in paradise."
—Luke 23:39–43

Everything in Christ astonishes me. His spirit overawes me,
and his will confounds me. Between him and whoever else
in the world, there is no possible term of comparison. He
is truly a being by himself . . . I search in vain in history
to find the similar to Jesus Christ, or anything which can
approach the Gospel. Neither history, nor humanity, nor the
ages, nor nature, offer me anything with which I am able to
compare it or explain it. Here everything is extraordinary.
—Napoleon

Mel Gibson's *the Passion of the Christ* is one of the most powerful
and incredibly intense movies that I have ever seen. It became a crit-

ically acclaimed global box office phenomenon earning over $611 million dollars worldwide. To make this movie as accurate as possible, Gibson chose to use the original Latin and Hebrew languages spoken in that time period. For me, it felt like I was taken back in time to witness what has become one of the most important timepieces of our history. This was far from easy to watch, as the true reality of Christ's suffering and torture was displayed with accurate intensity. It was almost as if I was the one causing his suffering and pain as I imagined all of my sin gathered up together at once and heaped on him as I pounded the nails into his wrists.

When I stepped into that theater to watch this rendition of Jesus's last twelve hours of his life, I was both terrified and mortified to watch the reality unfold before me. The suffering and sacrifice that this one man, Jesus, the Son of God, chose to endure in my place brought me to my knees with tears flowing full of shame and selfishness. I cried uncontrollably as my heart began to understand his true love for me in his torture and death upon the cross. I tried my best to prepare my heart for what I knew would be some of the most graphic and realistic visuals of what truly took place over two thousand years ago. I have owned this movie now for years, and I will be honest in saying that I have had trouble picking it off the shelf and watching it again.

This movie moved me deeply as it did to so many others throughout the world. I remember walking out of that movie after it was over, and there was not a word being said . . . not a peep. Humbled, crushed, silenced—my heart was broken from the truth of what Jesus went through for all of us. It only helped exemplify the depth of God's love for me. God simply and plainly shows us and says to us, "Look before you . . . my Son is nailed through his flesh and bone to a cross of shame so he can take upon himself the evil and the sin of this world, and because of *this* overwhelming love, you are now set free from your sins by the blood and sacrifice of my Son, Jesus, and through belief in him, you will have everlasting life."

I went and saw this movie in the theater twice. Each time, I experienced the same results, and each time, silence. I had read the testimonies of the Gospel writers regarding Jesus, his death on the cross, and his resurrection from the dead a hundred times throughout the New Testament. It was prophesied in Isaiah of the Old Testament well over six hundred hundreds years before this event took place in history.

There was nothing beautiful or majestic about his appearance, nothing to attract us to him. He was despised and rejected by men, a man of sorrows, acquainted with deepest grief. We turned our backs on him and looked the other way. He was despised, and we did not care. Yet it was our weaknesses he carried; it was our sorrows that weighed him down. And we thought his troubles were a punishment from God, a punishment for his own sins. He was beaten so we could be whole. He was whipped so we could be healed. He was pierced for our transgressions; he was crushed for our iniquities; upon him was the chastisement that brought us peace, and with his wounds we are healed. All of us, like sheep, have strayed away. We have left God's paths to follow our own way. Yet the Lord laid on him the sins of us all. "He was oppressed and treated harshly, afflicted, yet he never said a word. He was led like a lamb to the slaughter. And as a sheep is silent before the shearers, he did not open his mouth. Unjustly condemned, he was led away. No one cared that he died without descendants, that his life was cut short in midstream. But he was struck down for the rebellion of my people. He had done no wrong and he had never deceived anyone. But he was buried like a criminal; he was put in a rich man's grave. Yet it was the will of the Lord to crush him; he has put him to grief. When his soul makes an offering; he shall prolong his days; the will of the Lord shall prosper in his hand. Out of the anguish of his soul he shall see and be satisfied; by his knowledge shall the righteous one, my servant, make many to be accounted righteous, and he shall bear their iniquities." (Isaiah 53:2–11)

This is clearly and undeniably the most important fact of all that is in the faith of Christianity. If Christ had never picked up his cross, or if he had never risen from the dead early on Easter morning from this most horrific of Roman tortures, our faith would be nothing, and we would still be looking and waiting for a Messiah to come and save us all.

As I watched this movie, I knew that what I was seeing was a very close depiction of the incredible amount of mocking, pain, and deep suffering that our Lord Jesus chose to take upon himself. A suffering that most of us would not be able to fathom. How any man could have lived through just the floggings alone is a miracle. Imagine for a minute, what Jesus chose to suffer through for us—thirty-nine lashes with a led tipped whip ripping through the flesh on his back, buttocks, and legs all the way to the bone. Following that up with nine to ten-inch nails driven through his wrists and feet. This would be hard for anyone to watch and not want to turn their gaze away. But we should watch it, so we will all know the truth and reality of what kind of sacrifice Jesus chose to take upon himself for us all.

It is no wonder that hours before his arrest at the hands of Roman soldiers and temple guards, he was praying with a deep desire that his heavenly Father would release him from this final act. Jesus knelt down and prayed: "Father, if you are willing, please take this cup of suffering away from me. Yet I want your will to be done, not mine" (Luke 22:42).

What a tremendous amount of courage, it must have taken to live out his life with one purpose that he knew all along would eventually lead to the passion on the cross. How heartbreaking it must have been for him to see his chosen people deny him and cheer for him to be crucified, but for what? Why was he so hated and despised by his own people? So much so that they went to great lengths to have him arrested, mocked, tortured, and crucified.

In the richness of the four gospels, the biographies of Jesus's life, we see clearly the love that he shared and spread freely everywhere he went. He healed so many people of their ailments and diseases, and some of what these people were suffering with happened at birth. They had been carrying these burdens and diseases, pain, and suffering for years and years. Blind men born blind, men and women crippled from birth, lepers, deaf, and mute people who had never heard or spoke a word, a woman who had been bleeding for twelve years—all healed from just a word or touch from Jesus.

He would then turn the action of being healed upon the receiver of the healing, "Your faith has healed you, go in peace," pointing out to the one being healed the importance of *their faith* as a component to their healing.

To make his claim as the Son of God even more profound, Jesus brought three people back from the dead! One of them, Lazarus, who was a good friend of Jesus, had become sick and eventually died. Knowing full well that his good friend was going to die, Jesus purposefully took his time to arrive where his friend, Lazarus was. In fact, his friend had already been buried for four days when Jesus finally did arrive and brought back him back from the dead. In doing so, he could perform this breath-taking miracle in front of everyone who was following him and even to those who were not. Miracle after miracle, he did not hesitate to reveal his true identity by showing everyone the power he had been given by his Father in heaven. He was so scholarly that even the religious leaders and teachers were stumped by his ability to speak with such wisdom without any schooling or teaching.

I have spent most of my life searching, seeking, and studying the New Testament and the life and sacrifice of Jesus Christ. I am not even close to being a scholar, but I do consider myself a college student. Anyone can jump into the studies of the Bible or even pick a subject like Jesus Christ to thoroughly study and come to their own conclusions.

I accepted Christ into my heart when I was only eight years old. Over the years, I have had to ask myself this question: Do I really believe that I understood what I was doing at such a young age? To a point, yes. I even remember that day when I said yes to Jesus. I can honestly say that after I said that prayer, I was instantly comforted and felt a love overwhelm me. But in all reality, it has taken me a lifetime to come to the point where I am in my relationship with God, to feel I have something to share or even offer.

In all truthfulness and throughout my life, I have often prayed many times that people would see Jesus through me, not from my words, but from my actions. This has not, by far, been a favorable outcome for a good portion of my life. Within this life that I have been given, I have experienced what true unconditional love feels like, what grace feels like, what forgiveness truly means. Even now, the words I am typing into this book do not even come close to explaining in detail the power of what those words have meant to me in my life.

When someone experiences the deep impact of God's grace, his love, and forgiveness, in one's own life, that is when they have experienced the true transformational essence of God's supernatural desire to help someone change into a beautiful and loving human being and it is almost indescribable.

Let me pause for a moment to exemplify if I may, the truth. The definition of the word, "truth," "that which is true or in accordance with fact or reality. A fact or belief that is accepted as true."

All of us can claim that almost anything is true. I understand that this is possible, and many will refute my claims that Jesus is the one, true Son of God or that there is even a God. That is their prerogative. I can only claim what I have seen, have felt, have experienced, and what I have learned throughout this thing called life. I have taken in all the information, just like you, and examined all the evidence. I have doubted, questioned, and reasoned with all that I have come across on this journey of discovery—through nature, through life, through death, and everything in between. I have left no stone unturned.

You either choose to be open-minded and research what is available to us or you choose, for whatever reason, to be closed-minded and ignorant to what is available to us all. Let's take a subject for example. I have been fascinated with the Sasquatch since I was a little boy. Watched every movie and documentary that I could find. Read every book and studied all the evidence. In my final analysis of all the evidence, I don't believe that Bigfoot is real, but only a myth. To me, there just isn't enough out there for me to make a logical decision to say that this is a real creature living amongst us. Therefore, in my personal opinion, it is false, and untrue.

So this brings me to my next point. If you so choose to claim that neither Jesus nor God is true, ask yourself, "Why?" Why do I believe that? On what basis am I choosing to claim that he is not real or does not exist? If you truly have not put in the time or looked at the evidence, then on what basis, on what facts, have brought you to this final analysis in which you have chosen to believe what you believe?

I personally think that most people who have chosen to be a non-believer, be it an atheist, evolutionist, agnostic, etc., have not truly done their homework. Our sinful and selfish nature is always at battle with our soul. It is impossible to be human and not suffer with temptation and sin. It is literally already a part of each and every one of us when we are born. You cannot run or hide from it. Believe me, I have tried.

This actual truth is a tremendous burden to many. I allowed this burden of sin and temptation, shame and guilt, to haunt me for many years while not fully understanding what God's grace truly means. Not truly grasping the monumental act of the Cross. The Truth, that *I am No Longer Condemned* for my sins because of the blood that was spilled that day on Calvary.

I have counted the cost of following this man, Jesus. He even told us to count the cost and warned us it would not be easy. After years of my own personal study and investigation of this man who lived over two thousand years ago, I cannot and will not come to any other conclusion that in fact, not only is Jesus a part of our actual history, but he is undoubtedly a part of everything around us. He is alive and kicking, and Jesus is my whole life. There is a solid reason that billions follow him and have followed him throughout the centuries.

Do not doubt for one minute that there is not evil in this world. This is why Jesus came—to free us, if we so choose, from the natural sin and selfish ways of the world. He warned us how difficult it would be to go against the grain of this world. The world and all that is in it only wants to devour, destroy, and win our souls for the devil.

Many have claimed throughout history that Christianity will die, that Jesus will fade away and that the church is a joke. I am here to tell you, all of them, all of those people have been proven wrong.

Do yourself a favor. Take some time and do the research. Prove me wrong. But, even better, ask him yourself. Put Jesus on trial and look at all the evidence. There is a ton out there. I am not claiming perfection or that I even have this thing called life all dialed in. Not even close. None of us ever will.

The New Testament for me has changed my life in every way. Nothing has been more direct and more exemplified in my life than the truth and love that is written there in the words of the Gospels and books of the New Testament. Along with the Old Testament, the New Testament has been proven to be accurate with names of people, places, cities, and events over and over again through archaeology and our history, but more importantly, it has changed the course of history.

Have you ever thought about the fact that our history itself has been divided by the life and death of one actual historic man and the events that followed? BC and AD. What do they stand for? I am assuming that most people already know this—BC is Before Christ, and AD is After Death.

The history of mankind has been divided from these two most earth-shattering events in all of our human existence—the birth of Jesus Christ and his death on the cross. Hmmm? Seems like these must have been important occurrences in our history. Easter and Christmas are still today some of the most celebrated and cherished events in human history that are shared and enjoyed by millions every year throughout our world.

Yet, even in our history, in the name of religion and in the name of Christ, horrible atrocities have been performed and millions of lives lost because of it. Lest we forget, we are human and prone to sin and darkness, selfishness and greed, even in the false beliefs that what we are doing is right and falls in line with the Bible and Jesus's life and mission. We all have sin and darkness in us. It is a part of our DNA. This is why Jesus came to earth in bodily form, lived, and died amongst us, and was risen from the dead, so we could be saved from our sin and reconciled to God through the blood and ultimate sacrifice of his Son on the cross. We could not do this on our own. We do not have the will power nor the desire to be sinless. Nor would we choose to suffer as Jesus did and bleed for anyone in the way he did for everyone.

Our moral compass will hopefully point us in the manner that is good and right, truth and light. But we will ultimately fail, and Jesus knew this. His own disciples failed Jesus while he was with them! Jesus was constantly rebuking them for their lack of faith and failure to see God's good will and purpose. Sometimes, their own selfishness would rise to the surface, and Jesus would then have to set them straight with humility, rebuking, and correction. Jesus's most trusted and faithful disciple, Peter, even denied that he knew Jesus three times after Jesus was arrested at the hands of the Sanhedrin and religious leaders of his day. And Jesus had prophesied and told Peter he would deny knowing him three times! Yet Jesus loved him and told him that he was praying for him although he knew that Peter would screw up once again. Yet, Jesus also told Peter that he would build his church on the leadership of Peter, the rock.

> Then he asked them, "But who do you say I am?" Simon Peter answered, "You are the Messiah, the Son of the living God." Jesus replied, "You are blessed, Simon son of John, because my Father in heaven has revealed this to you. You did not learn this from any human being. Now I say to you that you are Peter (which means 'rock'), and upon this rock I will build my church, and the powers of hell will not conquer it." (Matt. 16:15–18)

Taking time to dig into the Bible is not only a chance to grow in your faith, but it is also a time to connect with God. I cannot tell you how many times God has reached out to me and gave me the words I needed to see, read, and hear at that one particular moment in my life.

God's Word is an open window to the freshest air you could possibly breathe. It is the wonder of the spiritual realm that is all around us but unseen. There is spiritual warfare going on for our very souls that we are unaware of but are constantly battling. Our relationship with God has to be nurtured just like any other relationship.

Let me make something absolutely clear here, right now. Religion is not what Jesus wants from us, he wants a *relationship*. Jesus was adamant and angry about how wrong the teachers of religious law, Scribes and Pharisees, were about their laws and sacred rituals that they worshipped instead of God and what he truly cared about.

> What sorrow awaits you teachers of religious law and you Pharisees. Hypocrites! For you are careful to tithe even the tiniest income from your herb gardens, but you ignore the more important aspects of the law—justice, mercy, and faith. You should tithe, yes, but do not neglect the more important things. Blind guides! You strain your water so you won't accidently swallow a gnat, but you swallow a camel! For you are so careful to clean the outside of the cup and dish, but inside you are filthy—full of greed and self-indulgence! You blind Pharisee! First wash the inside of the cup and the dish, and then the outside will become clean, too! (Jesus, Matt. 23:23–26)

God was concerned about love, grace, forgiveness, and mercy. All these pompous characters really cared about was lining their pockets with gold and silver and if they had the highest seats of honor at the dinner table. Should we not take a moment to look in the mirror at our own selves and ask how we are doing in these areas? I think best that we should be. If you're not checking yourself, then you are probably wrecking yourself, and you have no one to blame but yourself. Or you could go on with your life blaming your childhood, your upbringing, unanswered prayers, the lack of love, or the abuse, and use that as a reason to feel sorry for yourself. Blame your parents, or guardians of your dismal life . . . *wrong*, blame yourself.

You have a choice to make just like the rest of us. You can choose to let the things of this world and your experiences control you, or you can choose to empower yourself with the love of God and forgiveness of Jesus Christ. This is where the rubber meets the road. You are the captain of your ship, you decide where this ship will take you, nobody else. Like it or not, death is a part of life, and with death comes the reality of your choices and how you choose to live your life.

One day, judgment will come. You have been warned ahead of time. Jesus and many other Biblical authors warned us about the coming judgment. We will all have to stand before the judgment seat and be accountable for our words, thoughts, and actions. If your life was to end tomorrow, how do you see your life, your actions, and your words being judged? None of us is anywhere close to being perfect. We all have blemishes, stains, and marks. War wounds. What have we done to confront these blemishes and stains? Do you believe they have been washed away white as snow? Or have you been lackadaisical, selfish, and too focused on your own life to care? Dragging around behind you the sins, mistakes, and poor choices of your life like a heavy anchor drudging along the bottom of the ocean floor.

With all that Jesus did for us and all that he is offering to us, why is it we cannot seem to give him even ten minutes of our time and life each day? The depth of the love of Jesus is endless, his forgiveness never-ending. His grace is simply amazing. Once you capture these truths to the deepest part of your soul, you cannot help to be overwhelmed and speechless.

Therefore God exalted Him to the highest
place, and gave Him the name above all names,

> that at the name of Jesus every knee should bow,
> and in heaven and on earth and under the earth,
> and every tongue confess that Jesus Christ is Lord,
> to the glory of God the Father. (Phil. 2:9–11)

You have been examining the evidence your whole life—wondering and pondering whether this or that is true or even possible. Evolution or creation? Truth or Myth? Christianity or Atheism? Archaeological finds? These questions, broken down and dissected can be answered if you are willing to do the research. Throughout time and throughout history we all have been searching, weighing the facts, and questioning everything. But, we have also been letting what the world thinks—jam a wedge into the truth, and instead of finding out on our own, we believe the world first because that is the easy thing to do. That is where the road is wide, and you desire to please people more than choosing to love and please God.

> Jesus said, "Enter through the narrow gate.
> For wide is the gate and broad is the road that leads
> to destruction, and many will enter through it. But
> small is the gate and narrow the road that leads to
> life, and only a few will find it." (Matt. 7:13–14)

We, as human beings, will always gravitate to what is an easier path than to choose a more difficult one. But, there are no blessings down the path that is wide, no growth, and no change. I know, I have been there many times. I have only found deception, lies, cheating, pain, loneliness, dishonesty, disparity, division, brokenness with no healing, and hurt people continuing to hurt others with their painful pasts.

Until you have hit rock bottom, you will continue to believe you have this thing called life altogether. "I got this. I don't need anyone but me. I don't need your Jesus." That is also a very lonely road of slow destruction. The definition of insanity is doing the same thing over and over again expecting a different result. Yet, we, as people, will continue to sit and rot in our own feces instead of doing something about it. Choosing to make a decision that entails making a drastic change in our lives. Confronting the demons that have been tormenting us for too long. There has to come a time in our life when we just have to say, "I am *done!*" Done with all the lies that have been told both by us and the so-called ones who say they love us.

That's not love, that is deceitfulness, and that is brokenness. Until you decide to pull off the record that has been playing inside your head that is telling you, "You're not worthy," and allow Jesus to break that record into a million pieces, you will continue to hear the same song, and you will continue in your insanity expecting a different result. Life in all its beauty and love has *so* much more to offer. But you have to *believe in you,* and believe in the one that can save you, Jesus. You have to love yourself enough to forgive yourself and make a change. Allow God to heal you and start you on a path of genuine love, unconditional love, and forgiveness. Love that never ends and a forgiveness that will blow your mind and heart wide open.

Your heart becomes softer, and you are then able to forgive those who hurt you. With the simplest of terms, I am trying to reach the lost, the broken, the lonely and hurting, and the unworthy—the least of these. You are loved more than you can possibly imagine. Jesus wants to show you what that love looks like. He wants to shower you with his love and help you get out of the darkness that you have been stuck in. His forgiveness is real, and you are so very worthy of it all!

If it feels like you are being called by Jesus, I guarantee you, he is waiting with open arms. There are no tricks, no underlining message. This is not a gag or selfish motive. This is simply the good news of Jesus Christ who is offering you a free gift of salvation for your soul. If you want to know him like I know him, get on your knees and cry out to him. His mercy on your life is already there for the taking. He is not mad at you or ashamed of your life. He will not guilt you into anything. He loves you right where you are. To Jesus, it doesn't matter what you think you have done that is so terrible that you would feel unworthy, he loves you anyway, and *you are* worthy. His love conquers all fear.

Love is patient and kind. Love is not jealous or boastful or proud or rude. It does not demand its own way. It is not irritable, and it keeps no record of being wronged. It does not rejoice about injustice but rejoices whenever the truth wins out. Love never gives up, never loses faith, is always hopeful, and endures through every circumstance . . . Three things will last forever—faith, hope, and love—and the greatest of these is Love. (1 Cor. 13:4–8, 13)

He has a plan for my life and yours . . . "'For I know the plans I have for you,' declares the LORD, 'Plans to prosper you and not harm you, plans to give you hope and a future'" (Jer. 29:11).

When I was in Africa, I saw the lowest of the lows. People whose families had been wiped out by HIV-AIDS. Whole generations gone, just like that. There are over ten million orphans living in Africa right now. Approximately twenty-five thousand people die each *day* of hunger or its related causes—about nine million people per year. That is devastation. That is heart-ache. This creates a helpless situation for millions of parents in our world today. They can either watch helplessly as their children die from lack of clean water or they can watch them die from diarrhea and dysentery because the only water they can attain is diseased and tainted.

We live in a broken world who desperately needs Jesus. We need his love, his hope, and his forgiveness like never before. None of us have a clue when this thing called life is done. None of us have any idea what will happen tomorrow. There are no guarantees in this life. My life insurance is secured and written in the Book of Life, which is my true home—heaven with Jesus.

The absolute most important questions you should ask of yourself in this life are: "Am I saved by the blood of Jesus?" "Have I accepted his free gift of salvation?" "Is my name written in the great Book of Life?" If you are not sure, or it has been a while since you have had a relationship with Jesus, there is no better time than now.

And just so we have a clear understanding, you cannot earn your salvation. The work has already been done by our Savior, Jesus Christ, on the cross. We simply have to believe. That is our part—to believe in the One and only Son of God.

Doubts are a normal part of the process, we all have them, and that is totally okay. The journey starts here. He knows your heart, and he is okay with the doubts. Trust me, he will reveal himself to you, and you will never be the same. God created us to be smart and inquisitive. He wants our relationship to be on purpose, by choice.

Life is a trip. But it is just a blip, in time. I want eternal life. That life is *forever*, and I can't wait to see him face-to-face. I can only imagine! The words to this song, written by Bart Millard and performed by my favorite group, Mercy Me, have touched the lives of thousands upon thousands of people. There is a reason this song has gone Triple Platinum in sales. People are hurting, and they are searching for something to fill in the gaping hole in their chest where Jesus needs to be. Here are the words to this amazing and eternal song that reaches in and touches the deepest parts of our souls.

> I can only imagine . . . what it will be like,
> When I walk . . . by your side.
> I can only imagine . . . what my eyes will see,
> When your face . . . is before me.
> I can only imagine yah . . . I can only imagine.
> Surrounded by your glory . . . what will my heart feel?
> Will I dance for you Jesus? Or in awe of you, be still?
> Will I stand in your presence? To my knees will I fall?
> Will I sing Hallelujah? Will I be able to speak at all?
> I can only imagine, yah . . . I can only imagine . . .
> When that day comes . . . when I find myself . . .
> standing in the Son
> I can only imagine . . . when all I will do . . . is forever . . . forever worship you.
> —"I Can Only Imagine" by MercyMe

CHAPTER 7

DESIRES OF YOUR HEART

Teach those who are rich in this world not to be proud and not to trust in their money, which is so unreliable. Their trust should be in God, who richly gives us all we need for our enjoyment. Tell them to use their money to do good. They should be rich in good works and generous to those in need, always being ready to share with others. By doing this they will be storing up their treasure as a good foundation for the future so that they may experience true life.

—Paul, an apostle for Christ (1 Timothy 6:17–19)

By choice, I have lived most of my life on the edge. Always pushing it to the limits and seeing how far I can truly go. I know this is not the route most people would have taken, but for me, it seems to be the only way I knew how. As I have expressed before, I am an extremely passionate person at heart. The things that I have been passionate about throughout my life have usually become an important part of my life.

Since my brothers and I were born and raised in the Seattle area, we have always been huge Seattle sports fans for as long as I can remember. Throughout my childhood and into my adulthood, sports have been easily one of my greatest passions. I will never forget being glued to the television watching the Seattle Supersonics win the NBA Championship in the late '70s. My brother, Roy, and

I would get the sports section of the newspaper and cut out every single article on the Sonics we could find. In the '80s, the Seahawks missed going to the Super Bowl by one game, but then finally won it almost thirty years later. In the '90s, the Sonics were playoff contenders again and made it to the finals but lost to the Chicago Bulls. Stupid Michael Jordan (just kidding).

Then, in 1989, a kid named Ken Griffey Jr. got called up from Triple A baseball to play for our beloved Seattle Mariners Baseball team. Now that was an amazing time to watch baseball. I went to a ton of Mariners baseball games from 1989–2002. Unfortunately, now, I just don't have the time to invest in watching 162 games anymore. Life, a family, and work seem to get in the way a bit. But, I wouldn't trade it for the world.

Back in the '90s, it would be more accurate to say that I was obsessed with watching sports. I loved going to any of the games whenever I possibly could. I still do. One of my dreams has always been to catch a foul ball, or if possible, to catch a homerun baseball just like every other baseball fan who has ever lived. I would always get to the games two hours early, so I could watch batting practice and maybe have a chance to catch a practice homerun baseball. I definitely thought that I would probably never get a chance to catch one in a real game.

Before the game, each team gets time for batting practice and takes turns hitting the ball. A lot of those baseballs would make it out to the outfield where fans would be lined up with their gloves in hopes of catching a homerun souvenir. I was standing behind the railing over the tall right field wall, when the Kingdome was still around, hoping that I might have a chance to catch a batting practice homerun. I must have been surrounded by twenty to thirty people including kids of every age when Jay Buener hits a solid fly ball right to me, and I caught it. It was incredibly exciting! Then, about five minutes or so later, Buener belts another one, and I ran down the wall a bit, about fifteen to twenty feet, and amongst the other fans, I caught another practice homerun ball. Two homeruns in a row! That was a pretty exciting day for me, and I ended up giving one of those baseballs that I had caught to a young kid who wanted one as badly as I did.

I became a regular to those pregame batting practices and ended up catching quite a few of those homeruns. But in 1999, at the last game that was ever played in the Kingdome, my brother, Roy, gave me tickets to the game, and so, my son, Dalton, and I went. I had just purchased a brand-new baseball glove, but it was not even close to being worked in yet. No oil had been added, and it was stiff as a rock. Dalton had my old flimsy glove, and our seats ended up in right field where most of Ken Griffey Jr.'s homeruns landed.

As you have probably figured out already, I am a huge Ken Griffey Jr. fan. By this time, I had already been collecting his baseball cards for years, and he simply was amazing to watch. In his first ten years as a Mariner, he had already hit 376 homeruns, and now, at the last game ever played in the Kingdome before it was destroyed, in typical Griffey Junior fashion, he belts his 377th homerun . . . right to me!

There were two guys in front of me who were drunk as sailors, and they had no idea that there was even a homerun ball coming their way. So it came down to just me and the ball, and it literally flew right into my glove. All I had to do was stand up and put my glove out right in front of me and catch the ball, and my biggest dream would come true. I stood paralyzed realizing that not only was there a real homerun game ball coming at me, but this was a Ken Griffey Jr. homerun game ball, and I could do nothing but sit there and hope I catch it.

Well, as you might have guessed, I dropped it. It landed in my brand-new glove, then popped out, and dribbled down the aisle, three seats down from where I was sitting. It was then picked up by a rather large man with a huge Kingcup of pop in his hand. He valiantly stands up with the baseball in his other hand and raises it high in the air like he was swinging a sword in victory. If I could have, I would have grabbed that sword, sliced off his hand, and valiantly would have redeemed that baseball. Not really, but that is how I felt right then, at that very moment.

Instead of seeing a dream come true, I was experiencing in real life, a nightmare that I could not shake. To my absolute horror, I had just done the unthinkable. I was completely crushed, and I couldn't sleep for weeks after that. When I did, I would wake up first thing and remember that I dropped that Junior Homerun ball, which would then put me in a depressed state the rest of the day. It took me a long time to get over that missed opportunity. An opportunity I wish I had the chance to get back.

After that debacle with my "nice new glove," I made the next logical decision and plopped down over a $100 for a new Wilson baseball glove that was already oiled and nicely worked in. It was a thing of beauty, and I was on a mission to redeem myself. Anyone who knows me well, knows that I do not handle failure very well. I was determined that, if it was even possible, I was going to have another chance to catch a Griffey Junior homerun. A year later, Griffey was traded to the Cincinnati Reds, and there went my hopes of redeeming myself.

About two years later, in 2001, with Dalton again at my side, sitting in the center field seats in the front row at the brand-new Safeco Field, I was still ready for redemption. I came to every game with the intense determination that I was going to redeem myself and catch a home run baseball.

Brett Boone, who was the second baseman for the Seattle Mariners, was having an all-star year that year. He delivered a hit that became a line drive home run in the vicinity of where we were sitting. I watched that ball like a hawk swooping down to grab a trout and moved down the aisle to the left of our seats into the vicinity of where that ball was trailing off to. I lifted my arm as high as I could, and it flung my arm back as it entered into my mitt with a vengeance. I slowly pulled my arm down to look into my glove, and there sat the baseball nudged into the pocket of the glove all warm and cozy-like.

Needless to say, I was a bit ecstatic! In euphoric happiness, I raised my arms in the air like I was Rocky Balboa who just ran up that flight of stairs high-fiving everyone that was near me. I was just so overjoyed that my dream came true. While going after that baseball with such focus and determination, I knocked over someone's drink along the journey to get there. I was so determined to catch the next one that came my way I didn't see anything or anyone else because I never took my eye off that ball. I did feel like I had redeemed myself a bit, but I wasn't done, yet.

A year later in the exact same seats, but with my buddy, Bob Fuda, from Hostess-Wonder Bread, John Olerud, first baseman for the Seattle Mariners hit a bomb to the outfield, but this time to the right side of my front row seats. I crossed the stairwell to my right and into the next row of seats, clamored past two other guys and backhanded that homerun ball right into my glove. If I had not grabbed onto the front railing as I was catching that ball, I would have fell head first into the catwalk below. Those were good times! I guess you can say I felt redeemed. But even if I caught ten more home runs, I would have traded them all to have that one Griffey home run back in my glove.

Years later and two more children later, I had to let go of baseball, and so that leaves me with football and my beloved Seattle Seahawks. I love watching the Seahawks games, but they also stress me out! So, I have come to the conclusion for my health, and for the sanity of my family, that for me to watch them I have to record the games and then watch them later already knowing the outcome. I know that is sad, but it is better for my health and better for my children and my wife so as to not rip their heads off. My emotions become amuck with intensity and anxiety—which is not healthy. Some people will be able to understand and relate to me, and then there will be people like my wife, Lena, shaking her head and rolling her eyes at me because she thinks I am silly because I am.

My wife is just not a fan of Seattle sports, and that's okay, I still feel like I have found the rarest and most beautiful gem in my wife. I am so blessed and so fortunate. She is so supportive of my passions, and I support hers. She loves running in marathons, I don't. I hate running. We have to compromise sometimes in our relationships. My wife tries to understand football and all the rules and intricacies of the game the best that she can and even tries to sit down and watch it with me, but only because she loves me. I try and run with her for two blocks because I love her. Okay, it is more than two blocks, but you get the drift. Passions can be wonderful, fun, and fulfilling if they are used in the right context with a healthy balance and a limited amount of time.

Family time is so incredibly important, and our children need our attention all the time. Our kids, Anthony, Trinity, and my bonus son, Brock, are famous for saying, "Dad . . . dad . . . Hey, dad or Don . . . Don?" My wife always makes fun of this because when they are around, she can't get a word in edgewise. And so it is. I try with every ounce of me to give my children my time and my undivided attention. When they have something to show me, tell me, sing to me, or dance for me, I stop what I am doing and remember how badly they need this from me. This is healthy and in doing so makes them feel loved and important.

If your head is buried in a newspaper, the evening news, on Facebook, in a novel, or watching the Seahawks, just stop what you are doing, and give them some of your time. A loving and caring child only knows this because it starts in the home and this is what they have seen, experienced and learned. In fact, I believe children are nothing but walking sponges, gathering up information from every angle wherever they go. We, as parents, have to make our children our passion and our priority, or at least one of our most important passions.

Life is crazy and busy, I get it. I don't always succeed at doing this or even giving it my all, but I try really hard to. This is not what I received as a child growing up, so for me to implement that into myself as a father has been challenging. We tend to take on our parent's example when we become parents ourselves. Our job, as parents and adults, is to recognize our faults and shortcomings in ourselves, so we can improve as mothers and fathers to our children. At least this is what I have been trying to accomplish in myself and in my life.

Very rarely did I get my dad's attention, and it is even hard for me to remember my dad spending any time with me throwing the football around or playing catch with a baseball. Most of his answers were "Mm-Hmm" behind a newspaper or while watching TV in his tighty whities. He was great at getting us all to our football, soccer, and baseball practices and our games, but for him to take time out with us, just one on one, it was rare. Sadly, as I grew older, I always longed for his attention and his time, which never came to fruition.

When I was a senior in high school, I became friends with a guy named Gene Pennington. Both of us were a bit on the crazy side, and we would usually go out and do something stupid. Trouble was almost always not far behind. In the winter of my senior year at Mt. Si High School, Gene and I were working up at a ski resort at Snoqualmie Pass. On Friday after school, we would usually jump into my 1977 cherry red Gran Torino with bald tires and a hole in my gas tank and head up the mountain to work at the Snoqualmie Pass frying and glazing donuts. It was glorious work, and it was making a huge difference in many lives . . . not!

Our three main goals while working up there consisted of girls, beer, and fun. We bunked up with a bunch of other guys from high school in a room with one bathroom and one shower. You can imagine the smell of that place. Anyway, early one morning around 4:00 or 5:00 a.m., I had to get up, take a shower, and head downstairs to get started on making donuts for all those hungry skiers. After my shift was done for the day, I would do the same thing that everyone else was doing who wasn't an avid skier like myself: get drunk. Now, this was not something I was proud of either, but it was my way of handling life at the time and having fun. For me, it was also a form of self-medicating, which I ended up doing too much of.

Well, this particular evening after getting drunk and in my incredibly genius state of mind, I decided I wanted to have a pair of my own skis and poles. So, I trotted outside and began to look over all the nice pairs of skis and poles that had been shoved into the snow by the patrons who had stopped to warm themselves up and get a bite to eat at the Snack Shack. I chose a pair of skis and poles, plucked them out of the snow, trampled down the hill to the parking lot, opened up the trunk of the glorious Gran Torino, and shoved them in.

I, of course, was not exactly coherent as to who was watching and where. So I trotted back up the hill to the resort and because of the easiness in which I was able to just take what I wanted from the selection of skis and poles, I decided that my girlfriend at the time needed some too. So I plucked another pair of skis and poles, and again shoved them into the trunk of my car. Genius, I know. On my way back up, and because I was so smart and all, I decided that I needed just one more set of skis and poles for my best friend, Gene. Because I had never skied before, I was oblivious to the size of the skis I needed or if they were even the right size or not.

I was ready to head back up and call it a day, but on my way back up the hill from depositing the third pair of skis, I ran into one of my teachers, his friend and their two daughters, who I was very good friends with. They asked me if they could get a ride from the Snoqualmie Pass over to the summit, which was another ski resort, and of course in my drunk stupor, I agreed to take them.

So, we started back down the hill back to my car, entered the parking lot, found my car, and opened the trunk. Now after I opened the trunk and slowly realized that I had already forgotten that I had put all this stolen property in there, about ten people, mostly young men and women, surrounded me, my car, and my companions. They instantly got into my face and proceeded to accuse me of stealing all of these skis and poles—especially the ones that were theirs. I instantly became not only sober, but defensive so as to save my butt from getting kicked in all different directions. They threatened me and even said that if it wasn't for these men standing here with me, there would be pieces of me spread out all over this parking lot. And of course, I believed them. They took their skis and poles, and I played it off the best that I could telling them that they must have been put there by one of my friends.

Needless to say, it was a very ugly moment, and my heart was racing like crazy. The adrenaline was flowing, and I was thankful that I survived that ordeal as I proceeded to drive these poor bystanders over to the Summit Ski resort so they could get on with their journey home. As you can imagine, I was deeply embarrassed and did everything in my power to stay calm and just move forward like nothing had happened.

After we had all climbed into the Gran Torino, we started to slowly make our way out of the parking lot to the entrance. As we came up to the stop sign and were about to turn, we were then surrounded again by the same people who confronted me earlier and began to tell me that I was not going anywhere. They had called the police and then proceeded to tell me that I better turn the car off and get out. Of course, this is when my traveling companions decided smartly to get out and find another way to get where they were going. As they exited my car, they wished me luck, and as I watched them walk away, it was then that I started to feel as big as an ant.

I knew pretty clearly then that I was in serious trouble. As I stood outside my car in the dark of the night with snow falling all around me, I had the time to think about all the things that led me up to this one moment in my life where I felt all alone, humiliated, and in deep trouble. With all these guys standing around, looking at me like they wished they could rip my face off and to also make sure that I was not going anywhere, I pondered to myself why would I even do something like this?

To be painfully honest, I did have somewhat of a problem with taking things that were not mine at that age. My rebelliousness was a bit out of control, and my twisted philosophy told me that since I grew up poor and without, there should be no reason why I couldn't take a few things here and there. Other people were blessed with so much more, they have money and can replace these things. They're just things. But, of course, my moral compass was broken and needed some direction—some major tweaking.

Not long after I was surrounded, I saw the lights of three or four snowmobilers come shooting down the mountain to investigate what had taken place. This was the Ski Patrol. Then, just a few minutes later, the cops showed up and asked me to open my trunk, which I did. I confessed to my theft of this property and totally cooperated with them, so I could hopefully move forward and try to leave this mistake behind me. They didn't handcuff me, but they did put me into the back of the police car. He asked me like a hundred questions, and I was cooperative and willing.

Not too long after that, Gene came down, saw what was going on, and the story was out. Gene bent over with his hands on his knees to look into the police car to see me sitting there and just shook his head. Not out of disbelief or because he was mad or embarrassed. He shook his head because he knew very well that this could have been him sitting there instead of me.

After the police were done asking questions, they were contemplating what to do with me next. I was a week shy of my eighteenth birthday, and so I was still a minor. This information saved my butt from going directly to jail, which would have been in Ellensburg, about 30 miles from here. Instead, they took me to the nearest fire station and further questioned me there. They believed I was a part of some group or gang that was stealing skis and then turning them for a profit. I told them that I had simply gotten drunk and decided to try and pull off something as stupid as this. They eventually let me go, and I proceeded directly home with Gene by my side. On the way home and silent with my thoughts, I sat there examining my life, trying to figure out what had brought me to this. I had humiliated myself to the tenth degree with no way of hiding it or keeping it to myself.

When I had went back to school that following Monday, everyone knew about it, and it got even uglier. All I wanted to do was hide and hope this would eventually fall away. Even the teachers knew about it and made their feelings known to me. Teachers that used to like me now despised me, rejected me, and made sure to let me know how they felt about my delinquent course of action. It was a very difficult time for me, and I had brought all of this on myself. Most of my friends just made fun of me and some no longer talked to me. I knew this was big, and that it would have an impact on me and my life going forward.

About three months later, I had to go to court in Ellensburg and face a judge. I was sentenced to three years of probation and a $600 fine. That court appearance was the last scene of a movie about my life that I no longer wanted to remember. As I eventually moved past it and moved forward with my life, you would have thought that I would have learned from that experience. Nope, I didn't. As hard as it is to admit, I was still looking for opportunities to take things that were not mine.

Although I never got caught again, something changed in me one day to stop the deceitfulness altogether. I was working part time at Norm Johnson's Sports Card shop at Crossroads Mall in Bellevue. I would close down the shop a couple nights a week and had my way with whatever cards I wanted or packs of cards and just took them home. Then one day, it just clicked. What I was doing was not only wrong, but it went against everything I believed. This was not who I wanted to be.

I decided then, that day, I was going to make a change in my life and choose to never do this again. I grabbed all of the cards and things I had stolen from that card shop, walked in, and put it all on the counter, told them I was sorry for what I had done, and I quit my job right then and there.

I will never forget how it made me feel to choose to do what I did and to start changing the man I was into taking one more step closer to the man I wanted to be. It was like shedding a dead layer of skin. It felt refreshing and free. I had chosen freedom from this part of who I was, and I was able to put it all behind me and let it go once and for all. I forgave myself, and I moved on. The manager of the card shop was blown away by the choice I had made to return the stolen items. But this course of action is what needed to be done.

When Gene and I became friends, I had no idea what would become of it. We did have similar interests, and he was also brought up in an abusive, dysfunctional, Christian home with a divorced family just like me. We made each other laugh a lot, and we both were full of "piss and vinegar" in relation and in rebellion to our painful upbringing, but sadly, his story was even more messed up than mine.

After we became friends, I started to hang out at his house more often and I soon got to know his mom, Wanda, pretty well. She was a wonderful lady, and as a checker at I.G.A., got to know my dad because he would always go in and buy cigarettes from her. Now my dad was still married to Betty, who if you remember, was not a nice lady. Even though I no longer had to live with her, I still hated her with as much anger and passion as I could muster up. Let's just say that I didn't hold back on letting her know what I thought about her.

Those were days of extreme bitterness and fueled anger. I was at the peak of my rebellion and had no filter to speak of. As far as my relationship with Jesus at this time of my life, it is easy to say that he was definitely on the back burner. It would be at least a couple years later before I could come to the realization of how much forgiveness was needed in my life from all that I had dealt with. I was hurting and reeling from the pain of my childhood and this was my way, at the time, of dealing with it. Alcohol, stealing, destruction of personal property, and verbal abuse toward Betty—all signs of a lost and wounded child, but still, no one else to blame but me.

Now, one day while at Gene's house, his mom and I were talking about my dad. She eventually told me that she thought my dad was cute. Well, when I saw my dad next, I couldn't wait to tell him what she said. He then relayed to me some sentiments about how he felt about Wanda, and I gladly reported this news back to Wanda. Not too long after playing Cupid and relaying this delivery of flattering statements, I found out that Gene, his mom, and his sister were planning on moving soon into downtown North Bend from their current home near Truck Town, and they needed help moving. It just so happens that my dad had a truck. So, I recruited my dad to help Wanda move her stuff with his truck. He obliged and came over that following weekend.

As we were all working hard to pack things up and load the truck, Gene and I became hungry and decided to head to Truck Town to grab some food. Well, when we got back, Gene's mom and my dad had locked up the place and would not let us in. The rest was history.

Not long after that, my dad moved out of the house he shared with Betty and filed for divorce. I wasn't happy about the way it happened, but I wanted to see my dad loved and wanted by someone who would give him something he had never had. I had much to be angry about with Betty, and I knew deep down that his marriage to her was not right and not meant to be from the very start.

I longed to believe in real love. I longed to believe in marriage. That marriage was a good thing, a beautiful thing. So far, in my short existence on this planet at the time, I had seen nothing worthy of love, nothing worthy of marriage. I had only seen destruction, belittling, abuse of power, lack of love, and no laughter, no joy anywhere. This marriage that my dad and Betty had was not love, nor was it marriage. It was a farce and a jail sentence.

Finally, after most of his life of feeling unloved, unworthy of love, an unwanted failure, he was finally with someone who was perfect for him. Wanda made my dad's life complete and full. He laughed again a lot and smiled all the time. I had never seen him so happy in all his life, and I was very excited and happy for him. Wanda was able to give to my dad all that he had ever needed and wished upon for himself. To be loved and accepted for who he was—nothing else, nothing more. To be clear, I am not promoting divorce. Divorce is ugly and extremely painful. I would not wish that upon anyone.

My dad and Wanda became inseparable after that day he helped her move. She was his complete focal point and his passion. After the divorce was final, my dad and Wanda moved back into the house I grew up in—in Riverbend.

Sadly, my dad's new life with Wanda never did change a thing for our relationship, and I had to face up to that truth and swallow that sour pill whole. It was very bitter going down and only added to the fire of my anger and resentment. I had hoped that maybe he would now be available to spend some time with me now that he was free from his bondage to Betty. Unfortunately, my dad struggled to get beyond the outstretched arm of Wanda to spend any quality time with any of us.

You would at least think that the gratitude of it all would be enough to want to show appreciation for such a gift as this, and so it was. I again had to face the ugly truth of abandonment from a father that just could not be there for me. The hurt and pain of that truth was not fun to comprehend, and I simply could not make sense of it all. But, eventually, I had to come to terms with it, and years later, I had to forgive my father for what he had chosen to do. I had to forgive him for all that he did, and I had to forgive him for what he didn't do for me in my young life.

His passion for Wanda, his passion to be loved and cherished—which is what we all want, need, and deserve—consumed him and left nothing for anyone else. After my younger brother, Buck, graduated from high school, my dad cemented his feelings on his relationships with his family by moving to Mexico with Wanda. He never did want to get to know my son, Dalton, or spend any time with him either. It was simply a very sad gesture on his part, and a huge mistake in my opinion—a very hurtful and painful decision.

Passions have a way of sneaking up on you and even try to control you. This is why it is so important to continually check yourself. How much time is being consumed by your passions or hobbies? Have you made work or your career your passion? How much of your money is being spent on these passions? Is there anyone in your family that you are neglecting because of your hobbies, interests or passions? You have to be completely real and honest with yourself when it comes to this. It is vital to take a moral inventory of your time, your money, and your thoughts that are being spent on other things in your life. There is nothing wrong with hobbies, interests, or passions or even your career, as long as they are healthy and they make sense.

Too often, we invest too much into what we love outside of our own family. Or we spend way too much time and money on other things, material things, than on eternal things. If we could transport ourselves into the lives of people who are suffering to see firsthand what it means to be poor and without, I believe people would stop and ask themselves—do we really need this before buying it?

There is so much suffering from our brothers and sisters all over the world. "Yeah . . . but what can I do about it?" You may ask this question of yourself and maybe even say, "Can I really make a difference in someone's life?" The sacrifice is there for the offering. Everyone can sacrifice something to invest time or money into someone else who is in desperate need of help.

But even more importantly, we need to make sure we are spending quality time with our own kids and spouses. In fact, date nights with your spouse are not only vital, but are monumental to the success of your home, family, and your marriage. This should be number one in your plans to make sure your family is happy and healthy. Your first mission field should always be your family. Time spent here is absolutely the biggest investment you need to make—into your family, into your children's lives, into your husband or wife. They need you desperately, also. Again, this is your number one priority. There is a ton of wisdom in the saying, "Happy wife, Happy life!" Find out what your spouse's love language is, may it be physical touch, quality time, acts of service, receiving gifts, or words of affirmation. Always make sure his or her tank is full.

Sadly, most people who claim to be Christian, barely tithe the 10 percent that is being asked of us to give. We lack the faith in God to trust in him with our finances. Give 10 percent to the poor or to the church and you keep 90 percent. Seems logical and reasonable. But that is not what is really happening here. It is more like 1 percent of our earnings is being tithed. No wonder the rest of the world is suffering.

> Mankind wants glory. We want health. We want wealth. We want happiness. We want all our felt needs met, all our little human itches scratched. We want a painless life. We want the crown without the cross. We want the gain without the pain. We want the words of Christ's salvation to be easy. (John MacArthur)
> Let your light shine before men, that they may see your good deeds and praise your Father in heaven. (Jesus, Matt. 5:16)

As a Christian, Christ should be at the top of your passions, if you are truly believing that what you are is what you say you believe. To call yourself a Christian requires a lot more than just showing up to church on Sunday and putting check marks on a to-do list. It means to implement into your life the heart and mind of Christ. If you never open God's word and read it, study it, and chew on the truth that is in it, how can you know the heart of God? How can you expect any growth or hear God's voice or even know what your purpose is here on earth that God created you for?

This is not a lesson in guilt and shame that I am trying to show you. This is truth, life, and love. How much time do you spend with God? Are you just a pew-warmer, or do you get your hands dirty in the mud and sticks of Jesus Christ? I am not saying, "Go to Africa," unless of course God calls you there. There is plenty to do every-where for God's kingdom. Life is to be lived, loved, and shared. This is not a Han Solo act. A one-person play. Jesus warned his followers that you must take up your own cross if you are to follow him. Live your life for eternal reasons, not selfish ones.

"But whosoever will save his life shall lose it, but whosoever will lose his life for my sake will find it" (Jesus, Matt. 16:25).

As Christians, we are to be the example of Jesus—literally the hands and feet of Christ in our lives, in our families, and in the lives of others. We are to put into action what he called us to do and whatever that calling may be. We are to be light in this world and not the opposite of that. I am truly afraid for many who call themselves Christians just because they go to church every Sunday, pay their tithe, and walk out of that church never once looking to make a dif-ference out in the world. Saving face and marking boxes on a to-do list. "I have done my Christian duty, now I can do what I want to do because really this is all about me, isn't it?"

Every one of us needs only look in the mirror and ask a few simple questions about ourselves. To get real with the man or woman in the mirror ask yourself these questions: What are you doing to further God's kingdom? What are you doing right now to grow in your relationship with Jesus? Are you spending time with God in his word? Do you spend time in your relationship with him in prayer? Are you seeking after Christ with a zeal and excitement in your heart? Are you actively looking to find where you can make a difference in the less fortunate lives of others? Actions, not words, is what we need now! This is simply what Jesus asks us to do. His pain, your gain! It's time to pull our thumbs out of wherever they are stuck and do something. Make Jesus proud and add to your life treasures in heaven.

These things I have mentioned are not a to-do list. In fact, there is *no* to-do list. God does not want or expect us to follow a perfect organized plan, so we can make sure we are spending quality time with him and you can feel good about yourself. It is way more personal than that. I would fail everyday if I felt that I needed to follow a to-do list. And there are days when I end up not spending any quality time with God at all. He understands and just wants to be an integral part of your life. Not only that, but he wants to have a part in all of your life. To have this kind of relationship, and remember, this is *not* about religion, you must first seek him, to know him, and to love him passionately. He loves you passionately and only wants what is best for you and all of us.

We can never grow into the likeness of Christ, a Christian, until we choose to make him our passion. To truly know him is to love him, to worship him with all our love and appreciation. To love him is to truly live for him. To live for him is to give your life for him—all of it, all of your life and everything in it has to be surrendered to him. This is where Christ can finally move in your life and take you where he created you to be, your purpose. Then, Jesus can and will be your passion, your life, your breath, your vision, and your dreams can come true according to his will for your life. Please understand, this does not mean you have to become a monk and give up all the things you enjoy in this world. Along the way, you will figure out what is good and what is not in this thing called life.

One more thing that I would like to share with you is the incredible importance of understanding how wonderful and beautiful communion is. It is one of my most favorite things to do in my relationship with Jesus while attending service. To me, communion is one of the most beautiful and passionate ways of communicating and worshiping our Lord and Savior in such a personal and emotional experience. I cry every single time I take communion.

For those of you who don't know what communion is, it is the taking of one broken piece of bread and partaking in the drinking of the wine, (which is most always some form of grape juice, not wine). But what is most important is that this beautiful act is a representation of the Last Supper when Jesus broke bread with his disciples, and they drank from the cup he drank from. This is what it says in Luke 22: 19–20 (emphasis added):

> He took some bread and gave thanks to God for it. Then he broke it in pieces and gave it to the disciples, saying, *'This is my body, which is given for you. Do this in remembrance of me.'* In the same way, he took the cup of wine after supper, saying, *'This cup is the new covenant between God and his people—an agreement confirmed with my blood, which is poured out as a sacrifice for you.*

In this simple, yet elegant example with the bread representing his broken body on the cross and the wine his blood that he chose to shed for us, it becomes one of the most memorable ways that we can remember him and praise him for the solemn act of his sacrificial love nailed to the cross for us. This, the most unselfish act of unconditional love ever was for us—all of us.

It brings me to my knees in praise and fills my heart with incredible joy. This representation always humbles me to the full extent and understanding of his brokenness, his suffering, and his bleeding for me. He died for me, he suffered for me, and in a most glorious way, that love breaks down all the walls of fear and trembling.

For when I close my eyes and see him and know that he loves me that much, my heart rejoices, and it brings a great flood of tears, jubilation, and thankfulness to our Lord Jesus. "Do this in remembrance of me."

Thank you, Jesus, for everything. For your love is overwhelming, your patience and mercy for me unfathomable. My blessings are many, my sins are many, and yet, you still love me. Thank you for loving me, for showing me all that is in the world, and for helping me to see the things that break your heart. My life is yours, and I will love you always.

> "But the Holy Spirit produces this kind of fruit in our lives: Love, joy, peace, patience, kindness, goodness, faithfulness, gentleness, and self-control. There is no law against these things! *Those who belong to Christ Jesus have nailed the passions and desires of their sinful nature to his cross and crucified them there.* Since we are living by the Spirit, let us follow the Spirit's leading in every part of our lives. Let us not become conceited, or provoke one another, or be jealous of one another. (Gal. 5: 22–26 [emphasis added])
>
> Everything is pure to those whose hearts are pure. But nothing is pure to those who are corrupt and unbelieving, because their minds and consciences are corrupted. Such people claim they know God, but they deny him by the way they live. They are detestable and disobedient, worthless for doing anything good. (Titus 1:15–16)

To try and fathom or understand the fullness of God and his Son, Jesus, will be a never-ending study into the mystery of who God is. In a way, I love this. Not only does that leave us longing to continually seek out more and more truth, but it reveals to me that God is always in control. He will show you what he believes you need in your life right when you need it. He doesn't put all the Easter eggs in one basket. Nope. Like a great mystery novel, he keeps us on our toes, continually seeking him to find more and more truth and answers to this thing called life. And with that, I am extremely grateful. God is good, all the time!

CHAPTER 8

LIFE ON THE HILL OF RIVERBEND

Make new friends, but keep the old; those are silver, these are gold.
—Joseph Parry

A good friend knows all your best stories. A
best friend has lived them with you.
—Anonymous

At the tender age of five years old, I found out very quickly that life has a way of letting us know that there will be times when it doesn't seem fair, it isn't always fun, and people are just plain mean. As I have shared in earlier chapters, throughout my childhood, I had to accept the cards that I had been dealt without explanation or choice. Most of my days were filled with finding ways to just survive through the madness of our abusive, broken, and dysfunctional family. There were many days where the pain was so deep and the burden so heavy that I had to find some way, anyway to escape and cope with what was happening to me and around me.

I found refuge and escape mostly through playing outside, playing with friends, watching T.V., and listening to music. I was suffering through the effects of my mom disappearing, watching the pain that my dad was dealing with, and the hatred and wrath I had for a stepmom who chose to be wicked and unloving. I struggled with anger and bitterness watching a dad who wouldn't stick up for me or for my brothers or himself. He just allowed this woman to come into our lives and take complete control of it all.

Our family was forced to revolve around her and that which made her content. My dad eventually forced us to call Betty "mom," which I resented greatly. We never knew what kind of mood this woman was going to be in when we got home from school, and we also never knew when something would set her off. It was almost as if she enjoyed the power over us that she had been given and would abuse that power often. And if that wasn't enough, she tried everything in her power to persuade us to detest our real mom by telling us all the things my mom did wrong to my dad and to us in our lives.

At five years old, what I needed was love, affection, and an explanation to help me understand what was going on in my young life and why my life was being torn apart. I grew up very resentful, full of intense hatred, and bitterness but I didn't know how to release all that was buried inside me, and all that I had to carry from this part of my life. I tried very hard to find a way to love or even like this woman as a stepmom for my dad, but eventually, I couldn't take it anymore, and I rebelled against her with a vengeance.

I soon came to realize that no one else was going to stand up for me, so I would have to stand up for myself. I learned that I had to change the situation that I was in and no longer allow her to take away my joy or to control me in any way. Finding out later in life that she was bipolar answered some questions but still left a lot unanswered. This woman, who had introduced me to Jesus Christ, showed no signs of the love or light that should have been seen and expressed through her actions and words. Instead, what we felt and experienced were more along the lines of hard religion and legalism. Not relationship.

Around the age of twelve or thirteen, I began to rebel with a passion and take control of my own life, which seemed to only make her more furious and irritable and prompted her to try to control it even more. Betty was a large woman who weighed upwards of around 250 pounds but was only five feet and four inches.

So, one day, I was just sitting in a rocking chair, minding my own business when she suddenly snapped at me. At that moment, I was filled with so much rage that I could no longer take any more from this woman. So I stood up to her and told her, "No, I am done listening to you!"

She became infuriated, ran over to me to try and do what she had done many times before, and slapped me across the face. I grabbed her arm in mid-swing and then she tried to swing the other one at me to hit me, and I grabbed that arm too. While gripping her arms ever so tightly, I looked her straight in the eyes and told her, "You will never touch me again in any way." Then I pushed her arms back into her face, and that was the end of it. She never again attempted to hit me, but she did try in every way to continue to control me.

Most of my childhood and into my young adulthood, I had to fight against the feelings of intense hostility and wrath, but still believe and try to live for Jesus. I always thought that if I ever got into a fight, which I never did, I would probably pummel the guy so bad from just the malice and bitterness that was ready to explode inside of me. My only saving grace was living in one place in North Bend, Washington, which helped me build friendships that have lasted a lifetime. The two things that gave me hope, release, and a way out of my misery was my belief in God and my friends from the hill of the Riverbend neighborhood.

When I look back over my life and the extreme challenges I had to face at such a young age, I know that I survived because I was able to escape from my reality through the support and love of the friends I surrounded myself with and because of Jesus who never left my side. I was also able to see what a "normal" family really looks like from the families of my friends. I am fully aware that not every family is perfect, and every family has problems and issues, but the love of a family that is healthy and intact is so very strong.

After kindergarten was around the time I believe my parents split up and got divorced. We ended up selling the house in Seattle that I grew up in and moved to Everett, and this is when Betty entered the picture. From kindergarten to the sixth grade, we ended up moving five times until we landed in North Bend. Every time we moved, I had to say goodbye to the friends I had made and begin again to make new friends. I did enjoy the opportunity for new adventures and a new school, but making friends was not easy. My dad had moved us as far east as he could because he had found a job working at Darigold in Issaquah.

When we moved to North Bend in the summer before sixth grade, my dad had purchased a home on a hill in a housing development called Riverbend. Riverbend was a huge blessing because it had its own lake and a river running right by it with tons of forest to be explored. The lake had leaches, but we didn't care, and we swam in it anyways! We floated down the river so many times I couldn't even count. And when we weren't floating down the river, we were spear fishing trout or jumping off rope swings into the river. We built forts in the woods and traveled along logging trails where ever they would go to explore, and I was just thrilled to be living in a place where there was a good chance I could make friends and have adventures.

In Riverbend, there were three hills. The entrance coming down into the housing complex. There was water tower hill, which was popular in the winter for sledding, and then there was "The Hill," where our new home was.

I believe the first day we moved there, I was so excited that I wasted no time heading outside to go exploring to see what I could find. I remember it like it was yesterday. It was a beautiful sunny day with a warm wind with tall trees swaying ever so slightly. I decided it was time to wander up the hill and see what was up there. It didn't take long to find out that on this hill lived many different characters who would end up filling my days with some of the best memories I had ever had. If you haven't seen the movie *The Sandlot* or *Stand by Me*, you should because these movies are hilarious and very similar to what it was like for me as an eleven-year-old kid moving into the kind of neighborhood that I ended up in.

We never had a lot of money, and most of our clothes were hand-me-downs, so I guess you could say we were always on the border of being poor. I was still in that nerdy, weird stage, and with Betty cutting my hair, I always looked disheveled and was always sporting a bowl cut. My dad always seemed to be struggling with taking care of us kids and looking back now I can understand why. My dad never received any child support from my mom because she simply could not afford it. Betty would not drive or get her driver's license, so she never worked or had a job. Therefore, leaving my dad's income was all we had to survive on.

As I wandered up the hill checking out all the houses and yards looking for woods to terrorize, out of somewhere came that whistle that sounded like a catcall you might hear from a construction worker to a "hot broad" walking down the sidewalk. But I was no hot broad, I was just a skinny kid looking to make a friend. The whistler came from the back of a beat-up truck parked on a steep, dug out dirt driveway, right in front of a two-story house. Instead of one set of eyes looking at me, there were four sets of eyes that belong to the four kids looking at me with curiosity.

These kids ended up being from the Nykreim clan of North Bend, and over time ended up being my second family. There were four kids in the back of that pickup truck. Liz being the oldest, then Brita, Arnfinn and Kjell, the youngest—two older girls and two younger boys. Liz was a year older than me and Brita a year younger. If I remember correctly, we exchanged some "hellos" and "who are yous?" and then I was on my way continuing up the hill to do more adventuring.

Over time, I became friends with the Phinney Boys, the Braswells, Steve and Kris, and my next-door neighbor, Steve Haas, as well as the Nykreims. At the bottom of the hill and around the corner were also some more characters I became very good friends with, the Denunes, the Hills, and the Bozichs, which I am still friends with almost forty years later.

Over the next six to seven years, which seems like a lot more than that when you are that age, we would end up sharing together in some of my greatest adventures and memories with lots of laughter and a few tears. We all grew up together in that crazy time period before puberty and all the way through graduation from high school.

But as kids, we were always outside playing kick the can, baseball, tackle football, building forts, climbing and swinging in trees, snowball fights and sledding, trick or treating, running through the woods, riding our bikes everywhere, going over jumps, and playing lots of games. There were tons of birthday parties, sleepovers playing Atari into the early morning, and lots and lots of trouble.

Steve Braswell and I would raid the Phinney's house, consume all their food, and listen to records like Def Leppard's Pyromania, John Cougar's Jack and Diane, and Loverboy and Foreigner's Juke Box Hero while playing Uno or some other card game.

I remember when they had finally talked me into trying chewing tobacco. I was about fifteen or sixteen at the time. All these guys were chewing Copenhagen or Kodiac tobacco except me. I still don't know why they call it chewing tobacco because they're not chewing it, they're really just sucking on it and then spitting it out. I decided to finally give in to the pressure to see what the hubbub was all about. After I had put a dip in, it didn't take long for me to feel the effects of the tobacco, and I was buzzing like crazy, which they thought was hilarious. But not long after that, I was ready to pray to the porcelain gods. I thought for sure that I was going to hurl chunks, and I remember fanning myself with my t-shirt trying not to as my friends were laughing at me and enjoying the show.

Some of the other memories I have are when the guys bet me $5 that I wouldn't be able to drink a whole jar of dill pickle juice. In case you're wondering, I became $5 richer that day. I remember Kris Braswell and myself hanging out at the Nykreim's house all the time. Bev and Kermit, Brita's parents, would always be inviting us to dinner with them, and we would listen to the Rolling Stones, Led Zepplin, and Yes. We would always be getting into some sort of trouble, and we laughed a lot. Brita ended up becoming my all-time best friend growing up through high school, and we are still very close.

When I finally got a job at Thriftway, I saved my money, got my driver's license, and bought a car. My first car was a very classy and sophisticated car—a three-speed, manual transmission, two-door, 1976 Gold Chevrolet Vega with a white stripe down the side that said "Vega" on it. It was neither classy nor was it sophisticated, but it was a car. When I finally learned how to drive a stick, I grabbed some of the crew from the hill and we went for a drive. On the main drag of Riverbend, I tried to do a U-turn just after a curve in the road and ended up stalled and sitting right smack in the middle of it. I could not get the car into reverse nor could I go any farther forward.

This is when everyone in the car started to panic. Kelly Hill, Arnfinn, and Brita opened the passenger door and bailed out of the car while laughing and screaming at the same time in fear of getting nailed by an oncoming car coming around the bend in the road. I also panicked and finally got it into reverse just as a car was coming around the curve. I slammed on the gas pedal and speedily went in reverse into a cul-de-sac, but instead of staying on the road, I ended up sideways into a ditch. Now with the passenger door still sitting wide open because my friends had bailed, the door ended up folding forwards toward the front of the car like a hard-shelled taco as I was reversing into the ditch. I finally drove out of the ditch and was then able to get out of my car to survey the damage that had been done.

All of my friends were sitting there with their jaws wide open and mine was open as well! They would look at me then at the car then at me again waiting to see what my reaction would be. Then, almost simultaneously, we all just started laughing at how crazy this was and just happy that no one got hurt. My friends and I then attempted with some success to fold the door back to normal and then shut the door, which it surprisingly did. That passenger side of the car ended up being a Dukes of Hazzard type of entry from there on out with a huge dent in the side by the door. You either climbed through the window on the passenger side, or you got in from the driver's side. Good times!

I don't ever recall whatever happened to that Vega, but I became well known for trashing my cars. If I remember correctly, Kelly Hill and I went up into the muddy hills of Weyerhaeuser and took that Vega mud boggin'. I had that Vega in first gear the whole time while fish tailing around that mud and how we did not slam into the mud wall or get stuck is still a mystery, but man that was fun!

There were many other adventures like these that took place with my friends. One way or another, we always seemed to find a way to get into trouble. There was that day I stood up to Mr. McCarthy, and he chased me all over the neighbor's back yard. The insane night we all took Vivarin so we could all stay up late. Suppositories and vomiting pickle chunks the next morning soon followed that crazy scenario. There was the time that Brita and I decided to run late one night from North Bend to Snoqualmie after watching a movie at the North Bend Theater because we wanted to see our friend Lori. We threw snowballs at cars and jumped off every bridge in North Bend and Snoqualmie. I guess you could say, we were a little out of control. Little hellions is what we were. I believe though, we would never change a thing. Our memories, our craziness, and our times together were magical and everything we wanted them to be.

There was that one time I crashed my cherry red '77 Gran Torino, which Brita promptly named "the El Burrito," into a pond while trying to beat Liz's 45mph speeding record. This happened while I was driving down a certain dirt driveway through the woods that was about a quarter of a mile long. Driving as fast as I was down that dirt driveway and with so many curves in it I am surprised I didn't hit a tree instead. That whole experience ended up being rather difficult for us as we tried to get that car out of the pond without any parents finding out. Most of us ended up soaking wet up to our knees once we did finally get that car out with some tricky ingenuity. Out of the frustrations of our attempts to get the car out, we decided that each of us would take a swing with my thirty-pound car jack into the trunk of the El Burrito. It ended up with everyone involved carving our initials onto the trunk of the car next to our dents we made with the car jack. Memories. I wouldn't trade them for the world.

Yet, even then, I was learning how important my friends were to me. I found the solace, acceptance, support, and love from some of these friends that I knew, I would never find waiting for me at home. In fact, I never wanted to go home. My older brothers, Dave and Roy, were finding their own ways of dealing with the situation by rarely being there. They would be working, hanging with friends or with their girlfriends. If they were home, they would bury themselves in their bedroom with music that would drown out the reality of what was going on outside their bedroom walls.

Betty was a bit of an eccentric when it came to her religion. I will never forget when she tried to forbid Roy from listening to Lionel Richie because she thought it was Devil music. She may have introduced us to Jesus, which I will always be grateful for, but she messed us up with her own religious bigotry and hypocrisy.

My younger brother, Buck, who was six and a half years younger than me, was left to deal with whatever was left over from the wrath and craziness of his mom, which I always felt so bad about, and the fact that he had to handle that all on his own. Buck and I have always been very close. I believe that was due to the fact that Buck and I were the last ones living at home and having to deal with the home life that his mom put us through. All of us brothers ended up fairly close with one another. How we managed to grow and live fairly normal lives is a true testament to our faith in God.

One of my other friends on the hill was my next-door neighbor, Steve Haas. Steve was an amazing individual all by himself and always cared about everyone. He was also an entrepreneur. He came up with the idea of selling water before selling bottled water was even a thing. He would get a pitcher of tap water and go door to door and try and sell it. Genius. Steve didn't have a lot of friends on the hill, but we definitely became friends. On rainy days, we would each grab our knick-knacks, unwanted toys, anything we can find in our rooms that we could part with, meet over at his house, throw it in a pile, and play poker. Whoever won that hand of poker would then pick something out from the pile of goodies until it was all gone.

Steve was also my lawn mowing partner. A business we started together when I was about twelve to thirteen years old with my dad's beat up old lawn mower. We literally walked all over Riverbend looking for lawns to mow, and we mowed a ton of lawns. We had our little squabbles here and there, but Steve was a good friend, and we had some good memories together. When we would make some money mowing lawns around Riverbend, we would then ride our bikes to what used to be known as Tony's Golf Course and have cheeseburgers and shakes at the restaurant there. Sometimes, to make a little extra cash, we would go out into the woods near the golf course and find some golf balls to take to Tony who would then give us a quarter for each nice golf ball we found.

Around seventh grade, my brother, Dave, introduced me to Christian rock music like the group Petra. Petra was a Christian rock band that I became very fond of. I went to a Christian Youth group at Valley Christian Assembly in Fall City, and our youth group was going to take a bunch of middle school/high school kids to the Petra concert. I grabbed as many of my friends that I could for an opportunity to introduce them to Christ through this concert.

At the concert, they passed out buckets down each aisle so that after we had put our name and address on the piece of paper they had handed out to each of us, we would then drop that into the bucket. In the middle of the concert, they had grabbed all those entries and put them into an even bigger container so that the lead singer of Petra could pull out a name or two. Well, believe it or not, they ended up pulling my name out of the container, and I ended up on stage with Petra handing me a bag full of souvenirs such as an autographed picture, a poster and a Petra bandanna! There had to be at least five thousand people there, and those were the moments I believe God was trying to get my attention.

I tried as I could throughout middle school and high school to witness to my friends about Jesus. It was extremely hard, and it never went well mainly because I was struggling with my own understanding of what Christianity and a relationship with Jesus was all about. I only knew what I was experiencing at home.

Even though I had been going through hell at home, I still did whatever I could to make it the best childhood ever. And through most of it, I believe it was. When I got into high school though, that is when the real trouble began. I almost knew instinctively that if I did not branch out by being crazy, taking chances, and having fun then there would be a good chance I could go down a different path that would be dark and destructive. This is around the time that

Brita and I began to do things that most other kids would not dare do, which fulfilled my desire for the attention and acceptance that I was not receiving at home.

Plus, I believe our wild antics brought my friends and lots of other kids—joy and laughter that would also help them escape for a moment from their own troubled lives. I can only assume many lives were also filled with sadness, disappointment, and abandonment. I started to recognize that maybe I had found a gift by making others laugh with my goofy faces, impersonations, and getting in trouble while doing crazy stunts. This, for me, was the only path I knew of, so I took it. Looking back now in retrospect, this was another form of self-medication, in dealing with my broken and troubled life.

Some of my most cherished times was at Cedar Springs Bible Camp, youth group bonfires, and going to Mt. Si football games on Friday nights with my friends. I don't regret for one minute my choices to have fun and be crazy at times as a teenager growing up on the hill in Riverbend. Those were some of the best times I have ever had.

Life is a beautiful thing when you are blessed with friends. Never take them for granted the true and real friends you have and love. Find them, hold them, lean on them, love them, and hug them. Don't ever let go of those relationships. When life seems hopeless and home life is unbearable, don't ever give up. Trust me when I say that God has a plan for your life. There is so much more life to live once high school is over and this is when life really begins. Lots and lots of tears were spilled throughout my young life, but Jesus was always there with open arms even when I didn't fully understand what was going on. It seems to be what this journey of life is all about.

In this thing called life, we have to keep moving forward and reaching deep within us to never stop searching for truth and understanding. Life is full of challenges, pain and disappointment, trials and tribulations at every turn. There is no simple life. It is only as simple or as hard as you choose to make it. Failure is also inevitable and a part of the process. Hopefully, you will take what you have seen, learned, and experienced from your parents and choose to make the better choices that they did not make. You will fail, and you will make mistakes at every age, but these are the opportunities for growth, maturity, and understanding of the truth and reality of our actions and our choices.

If it wasn't for God in my life and his truth and love, I seriously don't know where I would be right now. I believe there is a very good chance I would have most definitely went down the path of drugs, or I would be an alcoholic full of rage and bitterness. I believe my friendships also saved me and helped guide me away from the things that would have been so damaging to me.

I can only hope that I may have been an inspiration and a light to others throughout my life of laughter, light, fun, love, and caring for others in my youth and trying anything to make us laugh to help us forget about the challenges a lot of us were dealing with at such a young age. I look back into my year books from high school, and I am grateful to read what others chose to write there in those pages. That, seemingly through my silliness and my willingness, I was able to bring joy, laughter, and a smile to those who needed it in some of their most difficult and dark times.

We *need* each other, we need our friends to confide in and verbalize our pain so we can get through this thing called life. We need to laugh at each other and with each other, and not take things so seriously. We are blessed to have each other and be there for each other. Comfort one another through the good times and the bad.

Life is truly beautiful, but for some of us, we may have to look a little bit harder to find it. I often wonder if those who have had to go through a much deeper experience of brokenness, a deeper level of pain and hurt, that we just might be able to see things more clearly and more vibrant because of our struggles. When life becomes beautiful and vibrant for the brokenhearted, it awakens in us a joy that we were desperately trying to find. This has been my experience in my relationship with Jesus.

When I fully understood the deep love and forgiveness that Jesus loved me with is when my life became full of light, joy, and pure love. I found out what true forgiveness really means. I found out what it feels like to let go of the hurt and the pain I had to endure at such a young age, to truly forgive the ones who hurt me. And that, my friends, was the start of my healing, my recovery, and the beginning of a new life.

I would like to take a moment to say a huge "thank you" to the Nykreims. This family has always made me feel welcomed, loved, and made to feel like I was part of the family. They helped me in more ways than they could ever imagine—family, love, togetherness, example, humbleness, and community. I love you guys so very much! To Brita, I can't tell you in words how much our friendship has meant to me all these years. Although we haven't had the opportunity to spend nearly as much time together over our adult years, our memories are simply the best and completely priceless. No one comes close to the fun, laughter, and craziness we shared together through those amazing years of our childhood and into our high school years. You taught me so much, and I am forever grateful.

To the Braswells, Phinneys, Hills, and Bozichs, I appreciate all the times you accepted me even when I was a bit quirky and off-balanced. You all kept me humble, and I have always appreciated your friendship. Especially you, Kris, I am so very happy we have remained close friends all these years. You were with Brita and me through a lot of our crazy and fun adventures. I appreciate your support, words of encouragement, and love over the years and in pushing me to write this book. And finally, the Denunes, we laughed a lot, and I thoroughly enjoyed watching you gals fight and pick on each other—hilarious and entertaining. This family was simply hilarious to hang out with. Oh, and thanks for pantsing me in your kitchen! Good times. Thank You, Mel, for your friendship, and being there for me from a distance always with a quick word of encouragement and love. You never gave up on me even in my darkest times over the years. Thank you for that.

Your friends can even be the rock you need in the most difficult times of life. The light in dark places. Lean on them when you need to. Look to them for love and encouragement through the hard times and through the dark times. I love all you guys so very much, and I cannot thank you all enough for all for the memories and helping me get through some of the hardest and darkest times of my life. There were so many other friends who I will always cherish who didn't grow up on the hill or in Riverbend like R.J. Canyock, Dan Davis, Kurt Stermetz, Kelly Gregory, and so many more. We had some amazing adventures as well.

I will always look back and smile and remember how much fun and how fortunate it was to grow up on "The Hill" of Riverbend. Memories I will cherish for a lifetime. My biggest suggestion for anyone reading this is to make as many memories as you can throughout your life, especially when you are young. Those years are but a blip in time and will be over before you know it.

Love everyone and never forget to think about what it is they might be going through at home or in their life. Don't judge others or be a bully just because you can or because someone is different than you. Life is already hard enough as it is. Choose to make friends and accept everyone where they are at. Stand up for those who need you, love those who are left behind, be kind, thoughtful, and generous. Befriend someone who looks alone. You just never know who might need you, right here, right now.

Take chances, live without regret and be adventurous, this is your only shot at this thing called life. Love it, live it, and enjoy it to all its extremes. Life is meant to be loved and experienced with Joy. And most of all, lean on Jesus and his unconditional love for you. Without him, I am nothing, and to him do I give all the Glory. Love to all!

"There are some people in life that make you laugh a little louder, smile a little bigger and live just a little bit better" (Anonymous).

"The most beautiful discovery true friends make is that they can grow separately without growing apart" (Elizabeth Foley).

CHAPTER 9

IF THE SHOE FITS

Live so that when your children think of fairness,
caring, and integrity, they think of you.
—H. Jackson Brown, Jr.

The greatness of a man is not in how much wealth
he acquires, but in his integrity and in his ability
to affect those around him positively.
—Bob Marley

Life has a way of bringing some of the hardest and most difficult truths to the surface of our lives. Sometimes, they can come from the most innocent of sources—like children for example. Children have a way of pointing out truths to us that no one else would ever dare say to your face. Not even your best friend. "Mommy, are you going to have a baby?"

"Umm . . . no, dear, why do you say that?"

"'Cuz you look like you are pregnant!"

The truth hurts. Of course, I have even done this at least once in my life. Assuming someone is pregnant, and they are not. So embarrassing. Children do have a way of just cutting to the chase and getting right to the point. They haven't developed their filter yet. And then there are people who seem to have never developed a filter.

They say whatever comes to their mind and speak before thinking it through.

Words, like a sword, can pierce a soul with hurt or fill that soul full of love. That kind of power is literally at the tip of your tongue, and what you say comes from your heart. I have experienced, as we all have, the damage that can happen from the words expelled from someone we love. From our words, we can choose to destroy or we can build up. But I also believe that there are times when it is absolutely necessary that an intervention must happen, which will deeply hurt the recipient, but if done right, will be done with truth and love. It becomes necessary sometimes, to intervene into someone's life with the words of this person's actions so as to hopefully put them back on track.

If you have ever experienced this in your life, an intervention, it is one of the most painful experiences but also the most beautiful. I refer to this experience as the Chrysalis Effect. This is what it must feel like to go from being a caterpillar to becoming a beautiful butterfly. I do also realize that even though there may be an intervention, it doesn't always mean that the recipient that is receiving the truth, through love, will choose to change into that beautiful butterfly.

Sometimes, the hard truths of our lives, choices, and our actions can be the most difficult to see and even believe that they are ours to claim. Once those truths have been brought to the surface and into the light, the recipient will usually become very defensive, even believing that what is being said is not only false but is also not a part of themselves entirely or at all. The recipient will usually shut down, shut out, deny it, and try to hide or run from the truths of the words being said. Or they will just fall apart, curl up into the fetal position, and cry like they have never cried before.

The truths of these words can be vital to the recipient as life itself. I believe throughout a person's life, there are many little interventions of truth that take place. It is up to that individual to decide to choose to either listen or not, to the truth being said. If you are bullheaded and stubborn like me, this will be an ongoing process throughout your life. But a necessary one. Filter in and filter out what is being said, and then choose to decide if it fits or not. Does the shoe fit with what is being said?

As I have said earlier, these truths, if said in accordance with the circumstances and with clarity, love and truth, not a selfish motive, can be some of the most important words you might ever hear. If the recipient can take into consideration the truths being said about themselves, digest them and process them, then they can possibly make a considerable conclusion that they are legitimate observations and therefore truth. Then that individual can choose to change his or her behavior going forward from the truth that has been exposed to them, or they won't.

I believe we are a constant work in progress—a never-ending work of art, or a Michelangelo that is in constant need of repair. We are creatures of habit and have the habit of doing the wrong things over and over again. I personally love the realization that we can change our behavior, our choices, and our lives whenever we feel that it is necessary. Growing can be painful, tedious, and even challenging to say the least, but necessary if your goal is to become the best you, you can possibly be.

If you choose to look into the mirror of your life and only see the reflection of yourself instead of everything else, or everyone else that is around you and behind you in that mirror, then you will be missing out on so much good stuff and so many good people. We, as people, easily get hung up on the negative things of our lives. We are too fat, too ugly, too skinny, too short, too tall, not smart enough, not athletic enough, not skilled enough, too slow, too fast, horrible this and horrible that. And this kind of thinking is pretty common amongst all of us. (Insert any negative thoughts here)

Some of our biggest challenges throughout life is to take steps of change which usually require courage, positive reinforcement, encouragement, and a belief in one's self. If we never take chances in this life, then we lose out on all the amazing experiences that life has to offer and the chance to grow.

One of my most, craziest experiences was when, at fourteen thousand feet, the side door of a plane opened, and I scooted my butt over to the edge of that open door, swung my legs over the edge, and looked down. That is the height of over three Mt. Si's on top of each other. I don't know if I can even put into words what that feels like when there is nothing between you and the sky—fourteen thousand feet straight down. It was the most exhilarating thing I have ever done, and I have done it three times! My wife has done it over three hundred times. Trust me, I felt like filling my shorts, but I knew this is what I wanted to experience, so that my life can be full and feel alive with adventure. The second time I jumped out of a plane my son, Dalton, went with me. I did a back flip out of the plane and it was awesome!

I know this type of experience is not for everyone, but it was the chance I wanted to take. I have always wanted to feel alive and feel that I have a purpose. I also have a feeling that most people, if they want to admit it or not, also want to feel that they have a purpose for being here, for being alive.

I even remember in high school telling my closest friends that if I ever acted like I am better than anyone else—slap me. I wanted to grow to be a man who lifted people up and not bring them down. I knew the depth of how damaging words can be to someone, and I never wanted to be that person who caused the damage.

There is a huge difference in choosing to intervene with truth and love than to feel that you are better than someone else and therefore feel the need to "change" them or "fix" them. Or even worse, wanting to change someone for your own selfish and personal desires. To become the man or woman you want to be, and long to be, takes determination, courage, patience, love, forgiveness, truth, and the willingness to change.

Years ago, I experienced an intervention that was not only unexpected but that came from the most unlikely of sources. After my second divorce, I was searching for answers—as we usually do after a dramatic change happens in our lives. I had thought that I had done all that was necessary to be ready for a healthy, happy, and fulfilled marriage at the age of thirty-four, but I was not. I was still a mess, and I still had a lot to work on.

Eleven years of marriage, two children later and now at the age of forty-five, I was again in the dark, and now I had to figure out how I had made a mess of my life once again. The truth hurts, but it also possesses a great opportunity for tremendous growth and reflection. Light, understanding, and growth can come from these dark times if we let it. I was reeling from the failure of my marriage, but always looking and striving to see the positives in it. I never wanted to be divorced in my life or ever put my kids on the same path of pain that I once had to walk and carry with me throughout my life. But, I also believed in the truth of love and that it was real.

When I married for the second time, I believed it was "till death do us part." Unfortunately, that is not how it turned out. I found out very quickly after we were married that I was not who I thought I was, and she was not who I thought she was, either. We did not give ourselves enough time to find out if we were compatible or even a good match. We rushed into the excitement of the thought and the dream of being married. Not a good idea, and I highly suggest you do not do what I did.

Marriage can be a very tricky thing if you haven't been honest with yourself or invested the time into yourself to do all that you can to be as healthy, balanced, and as ready as you can be. And I mean healthy in your soul, your heart, and in your mind. If you haven't prepared yourself for life, you are certainly not ready for marriage. Whatever you experienced in life and all that you have grabbed ahold of will be carried with you into the marriage, believe it or not. All of your hidden garbage, secrets, bad habits, masks, and baggage will be unpacked in that marriage. And if it is all unhealthy baggage, then it will have a direct impact on your relationship with your spouse and your children.

If I have any suggestions for anyone looking for advice before dating and before marriage, it would be this—do all that you can to heal from your wounds of your past. Seek out forgiveness to those who have hurt you, really forgive them, and forgive yourself for the hurt you have caused others in your past. If you can, and if it is possible, ask for forgiveness from those you have hurt. Then let it go. Let it all go. To look into the rearview mirror is to continually look for and feel the pain of your past. The past is called the past for a reason. Let the past be in the past. Look forward to writing new chapters of your story and begin new adventures. Forgive yourself and love yourself again. You cannot really love another unless you love who you are and who you have become. But, most importantly, put Jesus number one in your life. Your relationship to Jesus has to be the number one most important thing you work on first. That relationship has to continue to be the one you never stop seeking after.

There are two books I would highly recommend if you are in the dating scene or you are wanting to prepare yourself beforehand in looking forward to finding your soul mate. The book, *Date or Soul Mate*, by Neil Clark Warren is an amazing book for those who want to be ready for when "the one" comes along and also prepares you to put together the "Top Ten List" of characteristics that you will absolutely want in your mate and eventually in a husband or wife to be. It also helps you to see the importance of courting, dating, celibacy, and waiting for marriage to consummate.

The other book is called *the Five Love Languages* by Gary Chapman, which I touched on earlier in another chapter. This book is exceptional, and I believe is mandatory for couples who are trying to find out if they are ready to take the plunge into marriage. Are they compatible? Are there any red flags? One of the most important things to remember in this process is to be as completely honest and willing with the results of these books and to *listen* to them and the words they are trying to say. Don't make the mistakes I made when I flew past the "Red Flags" trying to wave me down and let me know that this woman or that woman was probably not the one for me. It seems that I have always had to learn that the hard way.

Please understand that even though, in retrospect, I believe I was not ready for marriage, I was given three beautiful and wonderful children in Dalton, Trinity, and Anthony who I absolutely adore and love with all my heart. I know that I am extremely blessed, rich in love, and family. God has a way of taking even some of our most painful and frustrating life experiences and making something beautiful out of them.

As you know, I grew up in a divorced and broken family. My intentions were to *never repeat* that scenario in my adult life and especially not through my own kids' lives. Every single day, my heart hurts for the pain I have caused them—*everyday*. I have had to live with those choices, and I also have had to fight to forgive myself every day. The evil one will always feed you with the guilt and shame card, trying to knock you out. He longs for us to be miserable and misguided. I have chosen to fight back with everything I have to give my children the best chance at a normal life.

I am not perfect. Show me someone who is. We all make mistakes, but that is why Jesus came, so he could love on us, help us to love ourselves again, and forgive ourselves and others for the pain that consumes our lives.

I think it is important to remember to never assume you understand someone else's life or marriage from the outside trying to look in. No one knows what is going on behind locked doors, and people have a way of always trying to save face by putting on masks pretending they are something else and they are not who they seemed to be. Brokenness takes on many different forms, and some are just better at hiding it than others.

Change must happen and change will come. Embrace those times of opportunity, and make the changes necessary so that love, truth, and honesty will be the dominant factors in your life. Take chances and take risks, but always try and remember to count the cost of your risk.

As I said earlier, an intervention came out of nowhere, and they usually do. I did not see it coming, but after the pain and the darkness of that truth, it opened my eyes to see the reality of my actions and my words. After the grief and mourning of my divorce, I was lonely and did not like being alone. I should have given myself more time to heal and recover, but I chose not to and jumped back into the dating scene way too soon.

How many times have you been given solid advice and then chose not to listen to that advice? We do it all the time. Maybe, just maybe, we should stop and really listen and take that advice to heart—especially from those who have been there and understand.

As anyone in the dating scene knows, it's not exactly the most pleasant of places to be. I tried online dating, dating people I knew and catching up with old friends who I once had feelings for— to no avail. As I continued on my adventures of being single, this should have been my opportunity to take that time to heal, reflect, forgive, get healthy, and I should have listened to the advice of others, but of course, I didn't. I was setting myself up for more pain and poor choices.

From the online dating scene, I had met someone, and we started to get to know each other. It started off really good and then got ugly really fast. I should have left when I had the chance but didn't. With red flags flying everywhere, I continued to stay in that unhealthy relationship because of my brokenness and loneliness—a poor choice on my part. As time went on, our pasts became more and more revealed, and the stories of my past became all laid out, like I was on the dissecting table.

The woman I was dating became more and more persistent in looking at the data she had collected on my life and began to unravel my story to highlight and reveal to me all my sin, darkness, and repetitive nature of my choices. At first, I was very defensive, eager to reveal her own mistakes so as to not make mine sound so bad. But in the end, she was right, I was every part the man she was unraveling before me, and I was disturbed at this revelation. Not only was she right to see this truth, but I was more embarrassed that I didn't see it first. I downplayed it, minimized it, made it an issue that everyone else was dealing with, and basically tried to discount it as minor. The dark truth of it all though would not go away lightly.

Eventually, the hard facts of my poor choices came rushing in to suffocate me and drown me in my sorrow. I had been called out on my crap, and I didn't like it one bit. As most interventions go, it wasn't pleasant, and it hurt so very much. I hated myself for what I had done. I allowed myself to make poor choices that hurt others and hurt myself.

I walked away from that relationship with my tail between my legs and never looked back. But after much pain and reflection, and a time of mourning over my poor choices, I would eventually recover from this to a new horizon and a new chapter. But first, I had to swallow the pain of my choices, the pain of my sin. I had to face the man in the mirror and ask, "Why?" I had to look at myself and ask, "What is wrong with you?"

This may seem like a goofy scenario, but it is actually quite healthy. Looking at yourself in the mirror and getting real with yourself can be a good thing. This process of mourning, grief, loss, sin, sadness, frustration of myself, anger, and hatred of myself, and the pain I had caused others was quite debilitating and humbling. I had to hit rock bottom. I had to break myself down so that I could slowly build myself up again.

This whole scenario went on for about a year or so as I completely cut myself off from all social media and deleted Facebook. I stopped going to church because I didn't feel worthy of God's love and forgiveness. I barely conversed with anyone for quite a while. It was myself and I, having to spend a lot of time working through my "stuff." Contemplating the how and the why of my life, the backstory, and eventually the reality of my choices—no one to blame but myself.

I had to literally start over. I had to find the good in me. I had to focus on who I truly wanted to be and to fight for that. I had to come to the harsh understanding of my poor choices and claim them, then forgive myself. And finally, kneel before our merciful Father to again ask for forgiveness because I am just a sinner who let his selfishness and his sinful desires get the best of him. Mercy, grace, love, and forgiveness—powerful stuff when you feel you have been given these things from God. My heart again was set free.

Of course, when you go through something like this, all of your other mistakes and failures become exemplified which becomes an even deeper burden to carry. Through it all, I had to keep doing what the Winter Warlock sang about in the Christmas Cartoon classic, "Santa Claus is coming to Town," "Put one foot in front of the other . . . and soon you'll be walking out the door!"

I had to pick myself up and start the process of healing and forgiveness. I had to come to terms with my mistakes, believe that these mistakes did not define who I was, and begin again to believe in the person I wanted to be. I knew deep down I had a foundation of goodness in me and that I needed to come to terms with my mistakes, forgive myself for those mistakes, and then find a way to ask for forgiveness. This would be the steps to recovery.

Slowly, I was able to build myself up again and begin anew. This time though, I left dating behind me and focused only on what I needed to do to get healthy. I chose to leave women out of my life completely until God felt it was time to bring that special someone into my life. My focus became only about my relationship with Jesus and his calling on my life. I needed to put Jesus *first* once again and stop thinking that I can do this thing called life without him.

A year later, I felt a calling on my heart to do another Save the Children yard sale, and my purpose reemerged. My life was no longer about me. Not about my selfish needs or desires, but about the will of God, my relationship with him, and what he created me for. I then chose to never again put people before God.

"Seek the Kingdom of God above all else, and live righteously and he will give you everything you need" (Matt. 6:33).

Time went by, healing took place, and purpose was restored. All by the grace of God, he walked with me through my trials and tribulations of life and for that, I am forever grateful. I cried a lot through that painful but necessary intervention. I thanked God for that revelation and that hard truth. And I was grateful for the person who revealed it all to me.

A little over a year later, I went on to build another Save the Children yard sale in 2016. In the process, I met my beautiful wife, Lena, who just so happens to have the same heart and passions I do for Jesus and for others in their despair. She reached out to me from New York, where she was living and working for the Air Force. Before we started dating, she wanted to donate to the yard sale by sponsoring a storage unit for six months, which was her tithing. She was being obedient to God and followed through with doing just that. We knew each other when she was still living here, and she also is a native of North Bend.

As we talked over the phone and Skyped across the country, we fell in love and were married six months later. We were fortunate over those months to have a lust-free courtship given the great distance between us! We both wanted to wait until we were married to consummate our marriage, which we did, and it has been the greatest blessing in our marriage.

God had blessed us greatly with an amazing relationship I thought I would never find—full of love, patience, laughter, and incredible intimacy, which I believe is a gift from God when you choose to follow his commands for a clean courtship and waiting until you are married. I highly recommend following the way God created relationships to be—courtship, dating, patience, obedience, and abstinence. We followed those two books I mentioned earlier in this chapter, and God followed through with his promises. Lena and I, we finally found what we were looking for. I certainly cannot say the same for U2.

A month before the big yard sale in June of 2016, I flew my two younger kids and myself to New York. Then Lena and I, her son and my kids, jumped into an RV and drove across the United States to come back to Washington State, put together this yard sale, and then in the month of August, get married. It was an incredible summer. In June, the whole family got to see Niagara Falls, the Badlands, Devil's Tower, Mount Rushmore, and so much more. In July, we had the Save the Children yard sale part 2 and raised almost $40,000 that went to build a whole bunch of clean water wells in Uganda, Africa, as well as help our local food banks, the House of Hope, and the Winter Homeless Shelter here in our own Snoqualmie Valley.

Life is hard. Life can be very challenging and very difficult to understand at times. We may not know why we are going through a trial or tribulation, but be reassured, there is a good chance you might be going through a transformation that you knew nothing about or even knew was necessary. We will all be challenged, and we all are a work in progress that never ends. Accept the changes that come as an opportunity to grow and become closer to the man or woman you long to be. Never forget that there is always room for improvement.

Learn to see the beauty that is who you are. You are unique, and there is only one *you*. Love who you are and forgive yourself for the mistakes you make for we are all human and are prone to make them. Give yourself some grace, look for the opportunities to seek forgiveness, and give forgiveness whenever you can. Life is too short to hold onto these things that only bring you down.

Wake up every day with an awareness of the gifts that have been given to you the moment you open your eyes to start a new day—life, health, to breathe, and walk, to see, hear, and talk. These are all gifts that we take for granted. To have a warm bed to sleep in under a roof that keeps you dry. Clothes to clothe you and food in your fridge and cupboards. Not everyone is as blessed as you. Many are trying to survive and may be living with a lot less. Children are going hungry every day and there are people who are suffering. We all have the choice to make a difference in the lives of other people if we so choose. This is life, and I hope we are all looking to find a way to make it a better one. I hope and pray that you choose to work hard to make you, a better you. Choose to make sure that the shoe that fits you is a shoe you would feel blessed to wear.

> Let us go right into the presence of God with sincere hearts fully trusting him. For our guilty consciences have been sprinkled with Christ's blood to make us clean, and our bodies have been washed with pure water. Let us hold tightly without wavering to the hope we affirm, for God can be trusted to keep his promise. Let us think of ways to motivate one another to acts of love and good works. (Heb. 10:22–24)

CHAPTER 10

FINISH THE RACE

The trophy that matters is not on our shelves or
resumes. It is the soul that we become. That is the
crown that we will one day cast before God.

—John Ortberg
When the Game Is Over, It All Goes Back in the Box

For God gave us a spirit not of fear but of
power and love and self-control.

—Paul 2 Timothy 1:7

It took me a little over three months to write this book from start to
finish. I truly had no idea how this was going to turn out. I just had to
believe that this was something God put on my heart that he needed
me to share. I have felt for quite a while now that this book needed
to be written, but for exactly what reason, I am not completely sure.
I wanted the words of this book to be read and understood to a depth
that would put a shock into your soul, wake the senses of your heart,
and hopefully open your eyes to see more clearly the love of Jesus that
is everywhere, all around us. I have tried very hard to touch on many
subjects that I believe are some of the most important factors of life,
love, faith, forgiveness, and happiness.

Life, I believe, is to be lived with a sense of urgency. Not in the ways of worldly importance, but in the truths that lie deep in our very own souls. Each of us are coherent enough to see through the murk and darkness of this world to the deepest underlining messages of love, purity, justice, faithfulness, truth, and our existence. The longer we choose to be ignorant to the truth of life and ultimate death, the longer we shall suffer in our own lies, deceit and sin.

Every Christmas, my family and I watch *It's a Wonderful Life*. And every single time I watch it, I end up sobbing because of the beautiful truths that are brought into the light. The messages portrayed in this movie are so very powerful. They cover subjects like suicide, greed, life not always being fair and predictable, death and mercy. But mostly, they reveal the beauty of community, love, forgiveness, and giving. This movie has an extraordinary way of helping us remember what is most important through this thing called life and that is being there for each other and loving each other through all the steps and challenges of our daily lives.

Because life has no guarantees, and can change on a dime, we have to constantly adapt to the ebbs and flows of what life ends up offering us. And yet, when bad things happen, we still ask the question, "How and why God, did this have to happen?" Whenever tragedy strikes, and tragedies happen every day, maybe, just maybe, there is a chance to change the outcomes of our tragic disparities. But to change what is, we have to first claim what it currently is not.

Until we decide that enough is enough, and until we, as a people, hit rock bottom, nothing will change. My only hope for this world is the foundation, with which I chose to build my life upon, the love and forgiveness of our Lord and Savior, Jesus Christ. I have come to find in my own existence and in my relationship with Jesus that we have many roads to choose from and to travel down. Each of us has to make decisions within our own lives that are literally life and death, heaven and hell.

Each time I feel a slight pain in my chest, I wonder to myself, "Is this it? Am I done? Is this when it all ends?" My dad died in the year 2000 from a massive heart attack while living in Mexico.

It didn't help that he smoked for over forty years. But I know that one day it will all come to an end. When? I have no idea. Only God knows. To me though, it is not the fear of death that scares me, but as a follower of Christ, have I finished the race? Did I fight the good fight? Have I kept the faith? Did I lead others to Christ by living as an example of his love?

Urgency is a word described as "importance requiring swift action." As fragile and fleeting as life is and has been clearly seen to be, I have felt a sense of urgency to achieve and experience all that I can possibly fit into this one beautiful life. If you don't see it this way, may I suggest you at least think about it and try to understand the concept I am trying to share?

I know you have heard this before, but we only get one shot at life. I have had the opportunity to taste the thrill of success. I have had the big house, the nice car, and I have had many victories that the world deems important. I have also shared with you my failures as well, but in the deepest realities of our hearts, true victory is accomplished through our loving, our giving, our compassion, our sacrifices, our friendships, our forgiveness, our purposes, our choices, our gifts, and our talents when they are done with eternal purposes. These things that bring about growth, maturity, and change in ourselves and the beautiful opportunity of helping others will also bring about these characteristics to our lives and to our hearts humbleness, joy, faith, integrity, passion, and a sense of urgency. This is where our accomplishments, our trophies, our treasures in heaven are stored.

Why is it that most of us, if not all of us, look in from the outside to admire and praise those who have come before us who have chosen a life that is outside themselves? A life of service, suffering, sacrifice of great cause, ultimate love, and purpose. We choose to praise and lift up people like Martin Luther King Jr., Mahatma Gandhi, Mother Theresa, Billy Graham, and even Jesus Christ, but yet, we choose to live a way that is not in sync to the lives they lived at all. Most of us are living our lives with one purpose . . . *ourselves*. We choose to only care about ourselves, our own wants, and our own needs. Our selfish motives and believing that the way to happiness is in the amount of wealth we have, power, toys, how big our house is, or how high can we climb the ladder of success within a company. All the while believing that if I can just have this title or that title, that is when I will have succeeded in life and then I will be somebody.

We have somehow become numb and accustomed to being a self-centered civilization of human beings all over the planet focusing on all that is deemed successful in the eyes of the world—only to limit, deplete, starve, kill, hurt, steal, destroy. and leave so many people stranded along the way continuously. There is no race or people, no category that is not exempt from these greatest of selfish sins and choices.

I have often wondered if I had won the Powerball Lottery, how challenging would the temptation be for me to become justifiable in my decisions in purchasing this or that. I have often hoped while in that daydream of winning the lottery, I would give it all away—that I would take that money and change the world. If I am being honest with myself, I believe I would invest most of it into saving lives, changing lives, and giving hope to the hopeless. I believe I would make the decision to give it all away. Would I buy a house? Absolutely! But a house that is the size that meets my most basic needs.

The transformation of the heart has to start with the realization that all this stuff, we think we need is *just stuff*. The cars, the homes, the vacations, and the money are all just stuff that we feel is so very important to our happiness, our joy, our fulfillment, or our definition of success. We think to ourselves, *I earned this, I deserve this, this is my reward for all that I have done in my hard work, accomplishments, and success.* Do you not realize how much of this success has been given to you by God? Is it possible that you are being ignorant to the reality of what God has given you?

We are just caretakers of his gifts. Prayerfully ask God what we should be doing with the gifts he gave us. How can I bless others? You didn't have it when you came into the world, and it will not be yours when you leave.

Consider the movie *the Dark Crystal* created by Jim Henson of the Muppets franchise. It is very entertaining and enjoyable to watch. In the movie, there are two species on a planet that have equal power and one of them, called the Skeksis, are very selfish, pompous, dark, and evil. They use their power to try and rule all the other species of creatures while the other equally powerful species, the Mystics, are humble, loving and giving. As the emperor and leader of the Skeksis is on his deathbed and literally going to die any minute, one of the other Skeksis is tempted and tries to take his scepter that is lying next to the dying emperor which implies great power and leadership. The emperor wakes up and grabs the scepter with a sense of force and authority, hissing at him, claiming over, and over again in a very sick and mutilated evil voice, "Mine . . . Mine . . . Mine!" Even to the brink of death and to the end of his life, his actions showed the importance of his title.

This has always been a definition or example for me when I think of people of power, or just people in general, who believe that their rank or title is what defines them and makes them important in this world. I have a good feeling that those who feel so very important are going to be deeply humbled. And those who are humble in this life will be greatly exalted.

"The greatest among you must be a servant. But those who exalt themselves will be humbled and those who humble themselves will be exalted" (Jesus, Matt. 23:11–12).

I have also had to come to this realization and truth. We all exalt ourselves at times throughout our lives. Some more than others. Throughout my life, Jesus has blessed me with many learning opportunities and experiences that have enlightened me and have brought about a deep humbling in me. A never-ending battle exists to choose to be humble over feeling that we are somehow better than others. I choose to be humble.

"Don't be selfish; don't try to impress others. Be humble, thinking of others as better than yourselves. Don't look out only for your own interests, but take an interest in others, too" (Phil. 2:3).

My hope and prayer is that people will be inspired from this book. I am praying that somehow I can inspire others to take a closer look at their own lives and take a leap of faith, to take chances, take risks, and hopefully see more clearly the world that is all around us. All of us are inspired every day by someone's act of kindness and their actions toward injustice or homelessness. We are moved deep inside of us where the heart is touched and the tears start flowing. Why can't that inspirational motivation come from you and me?

All of us, you, me, we can do something to make a difference in this world—a change in the direction of goodness, wholeness, purity, justice, and love. Let this become a part of your everyday life. *Do not* let fear become the only deciding factor to knock you off of your purpose and your dream of this life. Let your sense of urgency become more powerful than your fear. Get angry and fight against the fear, the hate, the lack of forgiveness, the abuse, or whatever it is you are battling against. Finish this race with an incredible story of triumph over evil, love over anger, forgiveness over hurt, and giving over selfishness and self-centeredness. Do not let the world tell you who you are or who you should be. Find your identity in the things that *conquer* hate, injustice, racism, greed, and evil. And if you haven't figured it out yet, find your identity in your relationship with Jesus Christ. He is the foundation on which to build your life that will guide you to forgiveness, hope, and love. He is the rock on which I stand.

The changes that will need to be made will not happen overnight, they take time and patience. In the words of the wise Jedi Master, Yoda, "You have to unlearn what you have learned."

Change the mindset of what used to cloud your thoughts into the mindset of what is truly important. If you want this bad enough, you will fight for it. Fight the good fight and run the race to win the prize. This is where the change happens, the transformation of your heart and soul. It will not be easy, but it will be the best choice you could ever make.

Getting angry at the source of what has been controlling you will help you to move past the obstacles in your life. Decide that this is it, *no more*! Be encouraged to take back your life and make it yours. Stop believing the lies you are listening to from yourself or others. Stop caring about what people think of you. All that matters is what you think of yourself and what God thinks. And I can tell you with a pretty good accuracy that God thinks you are pretty darn special and he loves you passionately. He loves you more than you could ever possibly imagine, and he has a plan for your life! I guarantee it!!

But, ultimately, all of this is up to you. You have many, many choices to make that will either lift you up or bring you down. It is up to you which road you choose to take. If you don't mind me saying, may I suggest that you take the road less traveled? Take the narrow road. The wide road is easier because it is of the world and the world loves those who fall into its trap. The world loves those who go with the flow, who don't rock the boat or go against the grain of this world and all that it loves—money, media, merchandise, sex, lust, pornography, titles, toys, selfishness, and success. The narrow road is a humble path of unconditional love, forgiveness, peace, acceptance, unselfishness, giving, mercy, and grace.

"You can enter God's Kingdom only through the narrow gate. The highway to hell is broad, and its gate is wide for the many who choose that way. But the gateway to life is very narrow and the road is difficult, and only a few ever find it" (Matt. 7:13–14).

Life . . . what a trip. Our history of the race of humans is a story of death and chaos, love and redemption, forgiveness and hate, wars and religion, blood and birth. We don't seem to have a clue how to solve our world problems, or do we? I believe we do, but the cloud of darkness, the evil one, will continue his reign of terror until the time when either Jesus comes back or our days on this earth are done.

The answers, which are very attainable, will always succumb to greed and evil in the hearts of men and women. What choice does that leave for the rest of us? Most of us are just peasants living in a world of dictators. Change will not happen until the hearts of men and women change. Not until their power has been stripped away, their greed, and money cut off and their hearts broken to the depths of the suffering in this world.

We all pretend we don't see it. We act like it isn't there. We turn a blind eye to the rest of the world that is suffering because it messes with our own agendas, our own selfish desires and goals. We make ourselves believe we don't have the power or resources within us to change what has already begun. That we couldn't possibly or actually make a difference in the lives of thousands upon thousands of children and their parents who are suffering and are dying every day. I can't sacrifice this or that.

Even in our own backyard, there is suffering, homelessness, and children who go to bed or to school with no food. I am just like you. I struggle every day to make sure I see it differently. I have to force myself to see it differently—out of sight and out of mind. This is *not* a guilt and shame fest. This is our reality of the world we live in. I am only stating what I see—the obvious.

I could throw up all sorts of stats, equations, and charts, but what good would that do? Change is what has to happen in our world. Each and every one of us has to find a way to make a change and to make a difference. Not only within ourselves, but within our country—this world. "I am starting with the man in the mirror, I am asking him to change his ways!" Michael Jackson even knew this to be true.

None of us are perfect, sinless, or without fault. We all need Jesus—all of us. I know there will be many who will choose not to accept the free gift of eternal life and forgiveness of their sins through the belief of God's only Son. This is what freewill is all about. Just like the lives that we have been given freely, freewill comes with that life.

To choose the life we live, the choices we make, the lives we touch or the lives we hurt and destroy, never forget—one day will come when we all will have to kneel before God and be accountable for all that we have said and done. The acts against humanity will be judged. And those of power who have abused it will be crushed. Many times throughout the Bible, there are warnings to us all, especially to the believers.

> Watch out that you are not deceived. (Matt. 24:4)
>
> As a prisoner for the Lord, then, I urge you to live a life worthy of the calling you have received. (Eph. 4:1)

Do to others whatever you would like them to do to you. This is the essence of all that is taught in the law and the prophets. (Matt. 7:12)

No one can serve two masters. Either you will hate the one and love the other, or you will be devoted to the one and despise the other. You cannot serve both God and money. (Matt. 6:24)

Do not store up for yourselves treasures on earth, where thieves break in and steal and where moths destroy. But store up for yourselves treasures in heaven where neither thieves break in and steal and where moths cannot destroy. For where your treasure is . . . there will your heart be also. (Matt. 6:19–24)

Not everyone who says to me, 'Lord, Lord, will enter the kingdom of heaven, but only the one who does the will of my Father who is in heaven. (Matt. 7:21)

The list goes on and on with many more warnings throughout the Bible. For those who have ears to hear, let them hear. Be careful how you choose to live your life and the choices you make. Always be looking in the mirror of your soul, searching for all the darkness that lies there so you can be rid of it. Live for Christ and his word. Follow his example and his commands.

"Love the Lord your God with all your heart, soul and mind" and, "Love your neighbor as yourself" (Luke 10:27).

This is the command of our Lord Jesus. We must be looking at every angle and in every corner to make sure that his light is shining brightly there. If Jesus is not your focus, then what is? If living for him is not your focal point, then what is? Accepting Christ into your heart is not a "Get out of Jail Free Card." It is not the Golden Ticket into Willy Wonka's Chocolate Heaven. Accepting Christ into your heart is the beginning of a new life—the old has gone, the new has come.

"Therefore now there is *no condemnation* for those who are in Christ Jesus" (Rom. 8:1).

Accepting Christ into your heart and into your life is ultimately the greatest and wisest choice you will ever make. All of us are asking the same questions, why am I here? How did this all start? Who made us? How is everything so perfect and delicately made? How did the planets come into existence? What is our purpose here? Are heaven and hell real? Is there really a God? We all have doubts, and we all have to answer these questions and come to our own conclusions. Through all the evidence that this world presents and has been found, we have to come to our own discovery.

Hopefully each of us will take the time to seek out the truth amongst the lies and do an investigation of your own from all the possibilities instead of taking them at face value. Your life and eternity hang in the balance of these truths and lies.

There is evil in the world, yes, but there is also good. To start with this premise is a good beginning. Why is there good and evil in this world if the world was made out of nothing, and it had no purpose to start with? If evolution is where it started, then why do we have any feelings or even care? How could something as complex as even our own bodies be constructed to the variable degrees to which they are, to the most delicate of details, and supposedly came out of nothing?

Do the research, ask the hard questions, and don't settle for what the world wants you to believe. Seek, and you shall find. My soul alone has felt the deepest penetration of the most overwhelming showering of love that I can't even possibly explain. In this book, I have tried to show you through my own life, stories, and experiences, what I have seen and heard. I have tried to paint you a picture of a life worth living of hope, of love, and a relationship that everyone can have if they so choose with Jesus Christ. I can only plant the seed. God must water it and cultivate it. You can't earn your salvation, it is a free gift. But, also, once you grow into the understanding of who Jesus is and your love for him and what he has done for you, you will want to do more and more for others because of the love, faith, and grace God has shown you. It is an understanding that only comes through the acceptance of Jesus into your heart and the ultimate gift of forgiving your sins and making you a new creation.

When it comes right down to it, heaven and hell are either real or they are not. This, like many other things in life, has to come down to the choice of the individual. Personally, like I have said before, I want to know now. I, like you, will not live forever. If this planet and all of its beauty is a small glimmer to what is next, I can't wait to see heaven. If you are choosing to be ignorant in believing that there is no creator God, then that is your choice and your freewill. Like many other things in this world, I have had a hard time understanding how people would not want to do the research on the most important topic in all of humanity.

How is it that a small ragtag bunch of Jews, who were being hunted and killed, were able to pull off and build the biggest faith in all of humanity? How is it that they put their lives on the line, supposedly for their faith alone in Jesus, and were able to spread and build a church based on the death by crucifixion of a man who supposedly died? Unless he truly rose again, showed himself alive to them, and is still alive today.

Why is it even to this day, we celebrate the birth of a baby boy who was born over two thousand years ago? Why is it that the Bible is the all-time greatest selling book? Why is it that our human history is based on and divided by the birth and death of Jesus Christ? How come four different global empires throughout history could not wipe out the Jews, God's chosen people? How is it that archaeology has helped to prove the Bible to be accurate over and over again? The questions go on and on.

My challenge to you is, will you step up and do the research and come up with your own findings? There have been more books written about Jesus than any other historical figure ever in the history of mankind. We have more historical documents on Jesus and the early church than any other historical antiquity in all of history.

The information that is out there begs of you to look into it and make your own case. You can either step forward or just sit still—your choice. Just remember that your life and soul are on the line.

My job here is done. I have shared with you all, all I believe that was put on my heart to say. Life is too short, the days too fast, and light will only be around for so long.

I will be half way to a century old next year and it feels weird. I feel like I am thirty, but I am clearly not. Twenty years will go by very fast, and then I will be close to seventy years old. A blip in time is all I am. When I am done and he calls me home, I can only hope that . . .

"I have fought the good fight, I have finished the race and I have kept the faith" (Paul, 2 Tim. 4:7).

May you love with the deepest of love, forgive so you will be forgiven, and live so that your life has purpose and will leave a huge dent in the world of the hurting, the starving, the lonely, the thirsty, the dying, the homeless, and the orphans. Let the wake of your life that trails behind you leave many with smiles on their faces, joy in their hearts, laughter in their memories of you, and love in their eyes. Love like no one is watching . . . but *Jesus.*

"Dear friends, since God loved us that much, we surely ought to love each other. No one has ever seen God. But if we love each other, God lives in us, and his love is brought to full expression in us" (1 John 4:11–12).

This is Godfrey, my sponsored child, wearing the
Seattle Seahawks baseball cap that I gave to him.

ABOUT THE AUTHOR

Don Baunsgard is a simple man dedicated to his family, community, and his relationship with Jesus Christ. He lives in North Bend, Washington, with his wife, and three of his four children still at home. Don enjoys photography, movies, hiking, and laughter with his family and friends.